VINTAGE

BEING MODERN

Gunabhiram Barua (1834–94) was a product of India's colonial modernity. He distinguished himself as an author, historian, editor and colonial administrator. Known for his progressive outlook, Barua wrote the first modern Assamese drama, which addressed the issue of widow remarriage. After the death of his wife, he married a widow and took a significant step towards women's education by sending his young daughter to study at Calcutta's Bethune School in 1878. His prose style greatly influenced the next generation of Assamese writers, playing a key role in the rise of modern Assamese literature in the late nineteenth century.

Banani Chakravarty teaches Assamese in Gauhati University. She has co-edited *Asamar Bhaṣha* (Banalata, 2013), part of G.N. Devy's acclaimed People's Linguistic Survey of India series, which has been translated into English as *Languages of Assam* (Orient BlackSwan, 2017) and into Hindi as *Assam Ki Bhashayen* (Orient BlackSwan, 2025). Her recent publication includes *Jetia Chapasal Nachil* (2024), a comprehensive anthology of medieval Assamese manuscripts, inscriptions and historical documents.

Being Modern

A Biography of
Ananda Ram Dhekial Phookan

Gunabhiram Barua

Translated from the Assamese by
Banani Chakravarty

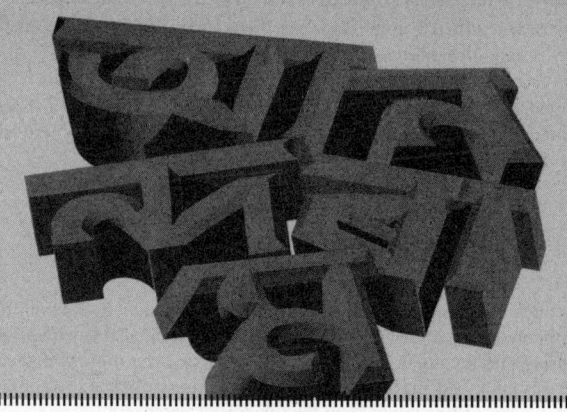

VINTAGE
An imprint of Penguin Random House

VINTAGE

Vintage is an imprint of the Penguin Random House group of companies
whose addresses can be found at global.penguinrandomhouse.com

Published by Penguin Random House India Pvt. Ltd
4th Floor, Capital Tower 1, MG Road,
Gurugram 122 002, Haryana, India

First published in Vintage by Penguin Random House India 2025

Translated copyright © Banani Chakravarty 2025

10 9 8 7 6 5 4 3 2 1

ISBN 9780143466352

Typeset in Adobe Caslon Pro by MAP Systems, Bengaluru, India
Printed at Replika Press Pvt. Ltd, India

www.penguin.co.in

Contents

Translator's Note

A century and a half ago, a young Assamese boy aged fifteen returned home from Calcutta with a boatload of new ideas and items, leaving his studies at Hindu School incomplete. He organized his life and home around these innovative concepts, which distinguished him from his contemporaries. However, unlike many of his peers, he also embraced his roots and traditions. This young man was Ananda Ram Dhekial Phookan. Born in 1829, three years after Assam was formally incorporated into the English East India Company's (EIC) territory, Ananda Ram would leave behind gigantic footprints in the making of modern Assam. The careful blending of traditional culture with Western modernity shaped Ananda Ram into the influential figure we recognize today. In his brief life of just thirty years, Ananda Ram achieved many significant milestones. Following his death in 1859, his illustrious life aptly became the subject of the first modern Assamese biography.

Just a few months after Ananda Ram's death, Gunabhiram Barua began publishing his biography in instalments in *Orunodoi*, the first Assamese journal published by the American Baptist Mission. This was eventually published as a book in 1880. Gunabhiram's biography is more than a mere recounting of Ananda Ram's life; it offers insights into the various phenomena that shaped nineteenth-century Assam. It showcases the cultural interactions between Assamese society and Western ideas, highlighting their influence and serving as an archive for understanding the era and its culture.

Ananda Ram lived during a time of significant transitions and witnessed the English East India Company's partial and final occupation of Assam in 1826 and 1838 respectively. As an official of the EIC government in Assam and a newly educated Assamese young man, he represented a changing world and exemplified the ability to confront new challenges. His remarkable intellect and enthusiasm make his biography an invaluable lens through which to view this transitional period.

Ananda Ram's family history is equally a testimony to the upheaval and chaos that Assam endured during the second half of the eighteenth century. It was an age of wars, mutiny and uprising, which caused repeated displacement of both commoners and kings. Laksminarayan Brahmachari, a wandering ascetic from southern India, settled in Assam and adopted a few orphans and destitute children, creating his new family. One of those children, Parashuram, eventually became Ananda Ram's grandfather. Gunabhiram, the biographer, was the son of Ranaram, another child adopted by Brahmachari.

Brahmachari, a shrewd statesman with a strong business sense, quickly rose through the ranks and became part of the inner circle of the Ahom rulers, eventually holding the position of customs officer at the Assam–Bengal border at Hadirachoki. His children inherited Brahmachari's skills and became very influential in both business and politics. Most of them permanently moved to Guwahati after the EIC took control of Lower Assam.

Ananda Ram's father, Haliram Dhekial Phukan, was an influential official in both the Ahom and EIC administrations. Haliram travelled to Calcutta, where he formed friendships with several Bengali orthodox elites. He was multilingual and authored two books in Bengali and Sanskrit. The Bengali *Assam Buranji* was printed at the *Samachar Chandrika* Press in Calcutta in 1829. After Haliram's death in 1831, Ananda Ram was mentored by his uncle, Jagyaram, as well as by a few EIC officials. Under their guidance, Ananda Ram went to Calcutta after briefly studying in Guwahati.

Ananda Ram studied in Calcutta in the 1840s and witnessed the intellectual and social upheavals of modern Bengal. He was associated with the Bethune Society and enjoyed the company of luminaries of the Bengal Renaissance. Back in Assam, Ananda Ram was employed by the zamindars of Bijni in western Assam and also by the EIC government. As the Dewan of the zamindar of Bijni, he drafted a comprehensive set of rules and regulations to govern the affairs of the zamindari estate, known as *Phookan Dewanar Kaydabandi*, around 1850.

Well-read in several fields of oriental and Western knowledge, Ananda Ram authored *Asamiya Lorar Mitra*, an encyclopaedic work for young Assamese learners, recognized as the first modern Assamese book written by an Assamese. Ananda Ram's vision of Assam becoming a highly developed province by following the economic trajectories of industrialised Britain found a prominent place in this work.

He also authored a comprehensive volume in Bengali on English laws applicable in India, along with an Anglo-Assamese dictionary that unfortunately remained unpublished and was lost, except for a few instalments published in *Orunodoi* following his untimely death.

Ananda Ram is usually considered one of the early architects of Assamese modernity. His role as an official of the EIC government was just as pivotal. Colonial officials recognized Ananda Ram's critical influence in the consolidation of the Company's rule in Assam. This was especially true in matters concerning the colonial government's efforts to decide Assam's revenue and land settlement policies. In 1853, Ananda Ram, then a junior official, prepared a long memorandum detailing his reasons for defending the *ryotwari* system of land settlement. Historians consider this one of the most significant moments in Assamese modernity.

A fierce defender of the individual legal rights of peasants in Assam, Ananda Ram's thoughts and actions had far-reaching impact on the making of modern Assam. Despite his short life, Ananda Ram engaged in many other experiments, including river training and agricultural improvement.

In 1862, Assam's commissioner, Henry Hopkinson, described Ananda Ram's intellectual position in Assam in this manner: 'Anundoram Phookan was as an Assamese, what Rammohun Roy was as a Bengalee, and looking to his opportunities and difference between Assam and Bengal, he must be regarded as even a more extraordinary man.' And yet, few readers outside Assam are familiar with Ananda Ram or his role in the making of modern Assam.

Equally overlooked is the transformation of Assamese society during colonial times and its close link with other parts of India, especially Calcutta. Though the Bengal Renaissance has been extensively discussed, its reverberation in Assam remains understudied. This biography of Ananda Ram fills this gap, shedding light on the scope and repercussions of this phenomenon.

British colonial officers and missionaries, both from Britain and America, played a significant role in mentoring Ananda Ram during his student years and beyond. His family background allowed him to form personal relationships with many such figures. This alliance with a section of the Assamese gentry was equally important for the EIC officials. Forging cultural links with these powerful families gave them the necessary vantage point to make the transition to colonial rule smoother.

Returning from Calcutta, Ananda Ram collaborated with the American Baptist missionaries, who had their establishments in Guwahati, to revive the rich legacy of

Assamese literature, which was largely overlooked by the Assamese elite at the time. This collaboration had many outcomes. The displacement of Assamese as the official language and its negative impact on education motivated Ananda Ram, who adopted the pen name 'A Native', to write a book titled *A Few Remarks on the Assamese Language and on Vernacular Education in Assam*. This work forcefully emphasized that Assamese is an independent language with a centuries-old, rich and vibrant literary tradition. It was intended to counter the claim made by Company officials that Assamese was merely a dialect of the Bengali language. For generations of Assamese scholars, this work remained one of the foundational texts of Assamese literary history.

Ananda Ram's Westernized lifestyle and close relationships with foreigners made him an outlier and unpopular among many orthodox elites. For instance, there was a whisper campaign suggesting that he was a renegade, which he vehemently denied even on his deathbed. Furthermore, some individuals advised his future father-in-law against accepting his marriage proposal. Gunabhiram also writes that Ananda Ram's appointment as an officer angered many members of the former Assamese aristocracy. Harakanta Sadaramin Barua, an elite EIC officer, did not mention Ananda Ram's name even once in his elaborate journal, published posthumously as *Sadaraminar Atmajibani*.

Fortunately, Ananda Ram did not experience any discrimination during his death rituals—a fate not shared by his son and other contemporaries. Gunabhiram's son,

Jnadabhiram, recounts how, after Ananda Ram's son Annadaram passed away, his family had to persuade a priest to perform the last rites by paying a fee of seventy rupees—an exorbitant sum for those times—as no one else was willing to do so because of Ananda Ram's open adherence to European customs. Hemchandra Barua, a prominent literary figure, encountered a similar situation. Jnadabhiram also states that Gunabhiram moved to Calcutta out of fear of facing similar societal backlash in his old age.

* * *

This biographical work is one of the most important contributions to our understanding of the making of nineteenth-century Assam and eastern India. A specimen of the emerging modern Assamese prose of the time, it often sees Assam through the lens of colonial Bengal's eastern frontier and narrates the life of Ananda Ram against the backdrop of contemporary Assam and Bengal.

The biographer, Gunabhiram Barua, was also a product of the same social milieu to which Ananda Ram belonged. Gunabhiram went to Calcutta to study and later joined the colonial administration. Inclined towards the Brahmo Samaj since his student days, he eventually converted to the sect and married a widow after the death of his first wife. In 1878, he sent his eight-year-old daughter Swarnalata to Calcutta's Bethune School—the first Assamese to do so.

He was a historian, literary figure and a pioneer in early modern Assamese literature. After shifting his base to Calcutta upon retirement, he became a guiding force for a young group of Assamese writers including Lakshminath Bezbaroa and Hemchandra Goswami, who later became pioneers of modern Assamese literature. As a close relation and ward of Ananda Ram, Gunabhiram had an intimate knowledge of his mentor. His proximity to Ananda Ram and literary flair made him doubly competent to be his biographer.

This fascinating biography, with its minutely detailed depiction of nineteenth-century Assam, has always been at the centre of scholarship on Assam. It is like a treasure chest—an amalgamation of oral history, folktales, official records, diaries and journals. Gunabhiram liberally used information from various sources such as *Buranjis* (medieval chronicles in Assamese and Tai languages), myths and oral history, besides his main source: the diaries of Ananda Ram. He also frequently used words from several other Indian languages such as Bengali, Sanskrit, Hindi, Urdu and Persian, sometimes adapting the spelling in his unique way in Assamese.

At the time Gunabhiram began writing his biography of Ananda Ram, most contemporary Assamese prose was produced by missionaries, and even texts authored by Assamese writers were often edited by them. However, Gunabhiram also drew inspiration from existing specimens of medieval Assamese prose, particularly *Buranjis*. This makes it difficult to determine how much of Gunabhiram's prose style in his biography was original and how much was influenced by missionary contributions.

In the standard literary history of the Assamese, the origins of Assamese prose have been dated to the sixteenth century. This prose style underwent significant reshaping and restructuring for modern audiences in the nineteenth century. Indeed, this period was marked by several twists and turns. Initially, American missionaries influenced the language by developing it based on pronunciation rather than on earlier Sanskrit-based spelling. They did this through the publication of dictionaries, grammars, translations, textbooks and, particularly, through the literary journal *Orunodoi*. The latter was published at the Mission Press in Sibsagar, Assam, beginning in 1846. The magazine was published continuously until 1868 and more intermittently until the 1880s. The publication of *Orunodoi* and parallel developments had a lasting impact on the modernization of the Assamese language in the nineteenth century. Ananda Ram and Gunabhiram's writing careers were deeply shaped by the emergence of these developments.

Among the different schools of emerging modern Assamese prose, Gunabhiram was considered the founder of one to which many younger Assamese writers looked up. Gunabhiram's sentences are short and crisp, weaving the story of Ananda Ram and contemporary Assam into a cleverly intertwined single narrative. His prose freely used linguistic elements from Persian, Sanskrit and Bengali, aside from pre-nineteenth-century Assamese. This text bears all the hallmarks of a master storyteller. It is a stylistic fusion of the *Buranjis* and modern narratives from other languages.

The absence of standard spelling and dictionaries forced Gunabhiram to rely on common sense and to spell many words phonetically. For the translator, this required poring through several language repertoires to uncover the intended meaning of a particular word— something of an elaborate cross-lingual puzzle. One of the challenges in this translation was identifying the original words, particularly proper names of items, books and people, sourced from English, Bengali, Persian and other languages, which were being spelled for the first time in Assamese. Gunabhiram had to adapt these words according to his preferred pronunciation. Often, it was difficult to determine the original spelling, especially for unfamiliar words of uncertain origin. Searching for these words in various dictionaries was often a tedious task. After an inconclusive search that lasted quite a while, I would occasionally find the correct spelling by rearranging the letters like a crossword puzzle. On other occasions, colonial government documents and glossaries proved useful. Gunabhiram often referred to British officials either by their surnames or first names. Identifying these officials was another puzzle. Decrypting legal or revenue terms written in Assamese or Bengali required support from various scholars.

Over the span of twenty years between the release of the *Orunodoi* version and the publication of the biography as a book in 1880, persistent demands from some young Assamese compelled the missionaries to adopt Sanskrit-based spellings. This shift is evident when comparing the two versions of the book. Alongside changes in style and spelling, the title of the biography also changed—from *Babu Anandaram Phookanar Jiban Britanta* to *Anandaram Dhekial Phookanar Jivan Charitra*. In 1915, Gunabhiram's son, Jnanadabhiram, released a revised edition featuring 'modern spellings' and 'minimal editing'. This version has been reprinted several times since 1971 by the Publication Board of Assam. In 2008, the latter published an English translation of the biography by Pona Mahanta and Ananda Bormudoi, based on the second edition.

The present translation is based on the first edition of the biography published by Ramanath Ghosh at Nutan Arya Jantra, Calcutta, in 1880. Archived at the British Library in London, this version was vetted by the biographer and published during his lifetime. I have read only five parts of the 1859–60 serialization in *Orunodoi*—the remaining sections have not been located. This made it challenging to fully incorporate all the changes made between the serialized *Orunodoi* instalments and the book version published in 1880. However, comparing the available instalments with the corresponding sections of the book reveals significant editing in terms of content, style and spelling. Ananda Ram's depiction evolves from a jovial young man into a more serious individual, and the narrative tone shifts from a leisurely, conversational style to a more formal, descriptive approach. This reflects not only tighter editing but also the evolution of Assamese prose as it began to move beyond the influence of American missionaries.

* * *

This biography was my first and only choice when I had the opportunity to translate an Assamese non-fiction text into English. It is one of the most widely read texts in Assamese on nineteenth-century Assam. I had been considering this project for a long time, especially during my doctoral research on the social history of the Assamese language in the nineteenth century. The text reads like a mysterious and complex landscape painting of Assam at the time. Translating it is vital for dispelling many misconceptions and confronting the widespread ignorance about the region during the colonial period. I therefore seized the opportunity to finally undertake this long-overdue task.

At first, I thought the translation would be straightforward, as I had read the text numerous times. It did not appear intimidating, and I believed I was well equipped for the task. My formal academic training was in Assamese studies, which gave me a reasonable understanding of both the period and the language. I estimated it would take no more than six months to complete, and I agreed to the deadline set by Ashoka University, which commissioned the translation. But I was proved wrong. The text turned out to be far more complex than I had imagined.

My aim was to translate every word without omission, remaining as faithful as possible to the original. I sought to retain Assamese idioms, expressions and rhymes as closely as possible. However, having taught graduate students Roman Jakobson's classic essay 'On Linguistic Aspects of Translation', I was aware of the challenges inherent in such an approach. I nonetheless chose to pursue this difficult path, despite knowing the limits of translating every word and idiom across languages and cultural contexts. I did not want to omit a single word penned by Gunabhiram, as each one felt like a treasure from that time. Even so, the challenges of translating terms from a century ago—many now obsolete—alongside numerous legal and administrative terms from other languages, presented serious hurdles. While I could translate each word into Assamese from the other languages used by Gunabhiram, I realized that these translations, although clear to Assamese speakers, might not carry the same meaning or resonance for readers in other languages.

A few readers of my first draft suggested removing the prologue because it seemed lengthy and disorganized, and might discourage readers from continuing. I was surprised by this feedback, as I had not noticed its length or tediousness during my multiple readings. I then realized that my familiarity with *Buranjis*, which use a similar style of arrangement—linking seemingly disconnected pieces into a coherent narrative—had led me to appreciate the biography's prologue more fully. The abundance of characters and actions throughout the text makes significant demands on the reader's concentration and memory. Additionally, it reads like a folk tale, incorporating myth, anecdotes and factual elements, and assuming a basic familiarity with Assamese society of the time. Aware that the text might lose much of its meaning and appeal for readers unfamiliar with the language and culture of that period, I began revising the translation by adding or omitting words where necessary, supplementing it with footnotes and restructuring sentences—sometimes splitting one into two or combining two into one—to enhance clarity and readability.

In this task, I unexpectedly received help from Gunabhiram, the biographer. I began to suspect that many sentences might have originally been written in English and later translated into Assamese. There could be several reasons for this. Perhaps, because this was one of the earliest modern non-fiction prose works in Assamese, it was easier to translate than to compose entirely from scratch. Gunabhiram was proficient in English, as evidenced by his legal judgments and petitions submitted to the colonial government. Moreover, much of the information in the biography was drawn from Ananda Ram's meticulously kept journals, which were likely written in English. This realization led me to approach the task of translation from a new angle: What English sentence might Gunabhiram have had in mind before rendering it into Assamese? It began to feel like a treasure hunt—trying to recover the imagined original English sentence from the Assamese version—and this approach often proved fruitful. Repeatedly working through idioms also helped, as many were likely translated directly from English or Bengali, a language that Gunabhiram deeply cherished.

Translating this biography has been an enriching experience, and it opened up to me even newer avenues and aspects of nineteenth-century Assam—something I hope the reader will share with me.

* * *

I am deeply grateful to Rita Kothari and Arunava Sinha of the Ashoka Centre for Translation at Ashoka University for this opportunity. I also appreciate the constant support of Diya Isha and Sanchit Toor from the Centre throughout the project.

I am honoured that G.N. Devy and Gautam Bhadra have kindly agreed to read a preliminary draft of the manuscript and provide blurbs for the book. I am indebted to Raziuddin Aquil from Delhi University and Anubhuti Maurya from Shiv Nadar University for their assistance with words of Persian origin. I also thank Prodip Khataniar, Prabir Mukhopadhyay and Rajat Kanti Sur for helping with names and dates.

I want to express my heartfelt thanks to my editor, Prashansa Taneja, for believing in me and offering generous and insightful feedback.

My gratitude extends to Elizabeth Kuruvilla and Vineet Gill at Penguin Random House India for guiding the publication process and offering their perceptive suggestions. I am indebted to Yash Daiv for being an exceptional copy editor, demonstrating understanding and boundless patience throughout the process.

I must also thank my students, friends and colleagues for their encouragement during this project, as well as my extended family for their support. I am especially grateful to Arup and Nizan, my family and conversational partners, for their unwavering support and patience. Last but not least, I owe much to Meewnu for being my companion throughout this journey.

July 2025,   Banani Chakravarty
Guwahati

A Note on Spellings and Conversions

This translation primarily adheres to a pronunciation-based transcription approach without the use of diacritics, except for proper names. In Assamese, the sound of 'a' at the end of a word is often omitted. Therefore, 'tarpana' is rendered as 'tarpan'. However, this principle cannot be consistently applied in certain cases due to the absence of equivalent sounds in English. For example, while the Assamese refer to their land as 'Axam', it must be retained as 'Assam' in English since the phonetic equivalent for the 'x' sound does not exist.

Transcribing proper names and surnames presents unique challenges, as many prominent figures have recorded their names in various forms including anglicized versions. For consistency, the most common and contemporary version of the name and surname has been chosen. The only exception is the subject's name, for which the original spelling used by him has been preserved. Additionally, several community names used by the author in the original text have been replaced with their endonyms, with the original references provided in the footnotes.

A more challenging task is determining the spellings of English and other non-Assamese names used by the biographer, as these often differ significantly from the original pronunciation. Frequently, consulting historical sources and researching names and surnames used by specific communities proves helpful. Additionally, proper names of books, clothing and other items from different languages present similar difficulties. The translation aims for accuracy by referencing sources in English, Sanskrit, Bengali, Hindi, Arabic, Persian and other languages, including vernacular vocabulary produced by missionaries and government texts. Current spellings have generally been preserved for names of places, rivers, states and similar geographical features. I have also used the older names for some places, such as Calcutta, to capture the essence of the biography's era.

The biographer employs both Gregorian and Indian calendars for dates, years and months. In the first half of the biography, most dates are presented as lunar dates according to the Saka calendar. In the latter part, two patterns emerge: either the Indian calendar or the Gregorian calendar is used or both are presented together. This inconsistency can make it difficult for readers to interpret the dates accurately. To enhance clarity and ensure uniformity, all dates have been converted to the Gregorian format. Saka lunar dates were transformed into Gregorian dates using the Jagjivan Ganeshji Jethabhai's *100 Years' Indian Calendar Containing Christian Samvat Saka Bengali Mulki Mugee Burmese Yazdejardi Fasli Nauroz and Hizri Eras With Their*

Corresponding Dates from 1845–1944 AD (1932), *The Bengal Almanac for the Year 1829, with a Companion and Appendix: Containing Phenomena; Chronological Information; Extracts from Acts of Parliament Relating to India; Bengal Military and Commercial Regulations; Regulations of the Public Institutions* and other reliable sources. The original text sparingly used a mix of Indian and Imperial systems of measurements for weights etc. Based on standard methods, these figures have been converted into the metric system.

For spellings and meanings, several dictionaries in Bengali, Urdu, Arabic and Persian from the Digital Dictionaries of South Asia repository of the University of Chicago were consulted, as were a few Assamese dictionaries, including *Hem Kosha* by Hemchandra Barua, *Chandrakanta Abhidhan* compiled by Asam Sahitya Sabha and *Adhunik Asamiya Sabdakosh* by Sumanta Chaliha.

Dear Annada,

I am dedicating this brief biography of your father to you, and I hope it can assist you in navigating through life.

While this book may not be perfect, it tells the story of an Assamese man who was a prominent advocate for the Assamese language. Furthermore, it serves as the first modern biography of our language. For these reasons, I hope that this book, despite its shortcomings, will be appreciated by both the literary community and general readers.

Gunabhiram Sarma
Nagaon
26 August 1879

Prologue

On 3 December 1779 CE,[1] Swargadeo[2] Lakshmi Singha, the king of Assam, passed away. His son Loknath Gohain succeeded him and assumed the name Gourinath Singha. Gourinath Singha was known for being very unpredictable and stubborn. He would not take anyone's advice, which made his reign authoritarian and harsh. He displayed extreme mood swings and a lack of common sense, leading some to describe him as mentally unstable.

During his reign, Gourinath Singha began to torment the Moamoriyas, who had been his father's enemies. He was also notorious for punishing minor offenders severely. A young man from the Mazumdar[3] clan, who had studied with Gourinath Singha, was blinded by the king for a

---

[1] The original text mentions the thirtieth of Aghon, 1702 Sak which may be converted to 3 December 1779 CE.

[2] Swargadeo was the title of an Ahom king who ruled Assam from 1228 to 1826 CE.

[3] The Mazumdar (or Mazinder) was a private secretary to the Ahom king, who composed letters to a foreign king and read out to the king the letters received from outside like letters from another kingdom.

minor offence. Later, when the king required someone to translate a letter from a foreign monarch—a skill known only to the Mazumdar—none could help him. He called upon the now-blind Mazumdar to read the letter. Unable to see, he could not read anymore. Another person helped him move his fingers over the words, which allowed him to decipher the message.

Afterwards, the king ordered his Bezbaruas[4] to restore the Mazumdar's sight. However, the Bezbaruas did not dare tell the king that it was impossible to put back extracted eyes. They instead told the king that only surgeons from the West could perform such a procedure. The king then dispatched an entourage to the West to search for these doctors.

* * *

In the south-western region of India, there was an ancient state called Dravida. A Brahmin named Bira-Raghaba lived there and had a son named Chandrasekhar, who, in turn, had four sons. Chandrasekhar was quite wealthy, but after his death, his sons were not as well off. The older sons were already married, and soon after, the youngest, Laksminarayan, also married and brought his wife home. However, unlike his brothers' wives, Laksminarayan's wife received fewer jewels and no nose ring. This situation

---

[4] Royal physicians in the Ahom kingdom who largely practised Ayurveda.

made Laksminarayan feel slighted by his brothers and insecure about their financial status. As a result, he became withdrawn and unhappy, fearing that his children would have a bleak future. He left home as a *brahmachari*[5] before the twenty-eighth century [sic],[6] accompanying an ascetic to holy shrines and other sacred places across the country until he reached Murshidabad.

* * *

Meanwhile, our entourage of surgeon–scouts also arrived in Murshidabad and docked their boat near the *akhada*[7] where Laksminarayan Brahmachari was residing. The locals were fascinated by the team's gorgeous long dhotis made of Muga[8] and Pat[9] silk, their bell-metal and brass utensils and large partition screens, as well as by their refined etiquette. Brahmachari inquired about the origin of our team, the purpose of their visit, and whether their state was under British rule. Our team explained that they were from Assam Kamrup, which was not under British rule, and that they

---

[5] A celibate saint.

[6] The year should be the eighteenth century. The present reference appears to be a printing mistake.

[7] A monastery.

[8] One of the varieties of silk found in Assam. Golden in colour, this silk, *Antheraea assamensis*, is exclusivly grown in Assam and was highly valued.

[9] Mulberry silk.

were searching for an eye surgeon who could transplant extracted eyes. Smiling, Brahmachari Baba said, 'Oh, that's why!' and pledged to accompany the team to Assam. He had already heard about Kamrup Kamakhya and wanted to take this opportunity to visit. He also thought the king was very foolish and believed he could make him understand that eyes, once extracted, could not be put back. Along with a few ascetics, Brahmachari Baba travelled to our country with the team.

In 1786,[10] Moamoriyas[11] caused chaos in Gourinath Singha's regime, leading the king to flee to Guwahati. Purnananda Burhagohain[12] *dangariya*[13] fortified the capital and defended it. People fled to different areas due to the Moamoriya's oppression. The king appealed to the British government for help, who deployed Captain Welsh[14] with some soldiers.

In Ujoni,[15] there was a prosperous village called Teok, where a few Brahmin families of the Gautam gotra lived.

---

[10] 1709 Sak.

[11] Moamoriya was the youngest order of the Vaishnavite sects in Assam.

[12] Burhagohain was one of the ministers of the Ahom king.

[13] Honorific for addressing a male noble, a minister and other high officials of the Ahom kingdom.

[14] Captain Thomas Welsh.

[15] The eastern part of the Brahmaputra Valley of Assam was described as such which is also referred to as Upper Assam.

They were well known as the Teokiya Adhyapak[16] family. Fleeing from the Moamoriya—or Moran[17]—uprising, a Brahmin from that clan escaped downstream on a boat with his wife and their eight-year-old son, Jogai. Owing to the turmoil in the country, neither farming nor trade was possible, and the displaced could carry little with them. The Adhyapak family had to survive without food for several days. The Assamese were addicted to betel nuts; they could survive without food, but not without betel nuts. Unfortunately, the Adhyapak family had none, so they had to endure without them.

One day, they anchored their boat somewhere on the Brahmaputra and, as fate would have it, some betel nuts and betel leaves were seen floating on the river. After taking a bath, Jogai's mother chewed those betel nuts. When Jogai's father returned from his bath and saw this, he asked his wife who had given her the betel nuts. She replied, 'I ate the betel nuts that were floating on the river.' Adhyapak became furious. 'You had betel nuts at a time like this, without knowing who might have floated them or why? I don't have any faith in you anymore.' He condemned her and sailed on his boat, leaving her behind. No one knows what became of that woman. Along with Jogai, Adhyapak and his companions took shelter at Asvaklanta[18] on the opposite bank of Guwahati.

---

[16] Pandit–scholar hailing from Teok in Jorhat.

[17] Moran is the name of a community of eastern Assam.

[18] A holy shrine in north bank of Guwahati, where the tired horses of Lord Krishna were believed to have rested for a while.

Captain Welsh arrived in Guwahati on 29 November 1792 CE. Krishnanarayan[19] and his men from Darrang had taken advantage of the king's vulnerability and caused havoc in the region. Once Captain Welsh arrived, the situation normalized. However, a cholera outbreak occurred in Guwahati, causing many deaths. This was followed by an epidemic of diarrhoea, which was equally fatal. Laksminarayan arrived in Guwahati during this time, but the issue of the eye transplant did not arise, as the blind Mazumdar had already passed away.

Brahmachari, being a medical expert, successfully treated many patients suffering from diarrhoea. Opium cultivation and usage began in the country during this period. Poppy seeds for cultivation were procured from soldiers and others coming from the West. Opium was a primary medicine to treat cholera and diarrhoea, and the local people accepted it enthusiastically.

Captain Welsh went up to Rangpur with the king and his soldiers, and Brahmachari accompanied them after visiting Kamakhya and other shrines. Following the defeat of the Moamoriyas and the king's reinstatement, Captain Welsh returned in the month of Chot[20] in 1793. Brahmachari became a favourite of the king, the prime minister and other officials due to his intelligence and foresight. As there was a shortage of skilled soldiers in the country, Brahmachari promised to arrange for Sikh and

---

[19] The Koch king of Darrang.

[20] March–April.

Hindustani men to join the king's army. Some soldiers he eventually brought remained in Assam, while others were stationed in Hadirachoki or Bongalhat, the Assam–Bengal border. Paka Beji, the Duworiya Barua[21] at that time, became a Mahanta[22] with the king's permission. His family is still celebrated as the Gosains of Bamundi.[23] Brahmachari persuaded the king and Burhagohain to make him the new Duworiya Barua. Brahmachari sometimes stayed at Bonagalhat Hadira, sometimes at Nilachal Hill in Guwahati and sometimes in the capital. His base in Guwahati was known as the old camp.

Brahmachari set up a Shiva[24] shrine on a hill in Phulara village near Hadira and arranged for the deity's worship. He also transformed his home into a temple by installing idols of Gopal, Ganesh and other gods, and by collecting many Shaligrams.[25]

Jogai's father, a member of the Teokiya Adhyapak clan, passed away at Asvaklanta. After his death, Jogai became an orphan and was taken in by Laksminarayan Brahmachari, who became his mentor. When Jogai's family in Teok learnt about his parents' situation, a few of them came to

---

[21] The officer incharge of the custom check point in the western border of the Ahom kingdom.

[22] A Vaishavite religious preacher.

[23] Religious preachers from Bamundi, a place near Guwahati.

[24] Either an idol or a Shivalinga dedicated to the Hindu God Shiva.

[25] A fossil ammonite held by the Hindus to be representative of Lord Vishnu.

inquire about him. One of Jogai's cousins, who was slightly older than him and also an orphan, accompanied them. Brahmachari accepted him too.

Brahmachari also cared for two other orphaned Brahmin boys from Kamrup. A Brahmin widow from Kamrup, who had two young sons, was also taken in by Brahmachari. In addition to adopting her sons, he adopted an orphaned Brahmin girl and treated her as his daughter. He provided shelter to the widow so she could look after all the children. He built an independent house for them and called the Brahmin widow 'Dukhu's mother'.

Brahmachari renamed all the boys. The eldest became Sitaram; the next, from Teok, was named Parashuram. The third was named Shambhuram, and Jogai was renamed Ranaram. The elder son of Dukhu's mother became Abhiram, and the younger was named Patabhiram. The daughter got the name Patoli. Brahmachari organized the sacred thread ceremony for Sitaram, Parashuram and Shambhuram, initiating them into his gotra.[26] Similarly, Sitaram initiated Abhiram; Parashuram initiated Ranaram; and Shambhuram initiated Patabhiram. All of them became brothers thereafter. They now belonged to the Srivatsya gotra, just like Brahmachari. The family became direct descendants of Bhargava, Chyavana, Apnuvana, Aurva and Jamadagni.[27] They stopped following the daily

---

[26] A Hindu clan tracing its paternal lineage from a common ancestor, usually a saint or sage.

[27] These saints were the ancestors belonging to the Srivatsya gotra.

rituals prevalent in Assam and adopted the Dravidian Sandhya[28] system for rituals. However, they still followed the Yajurveda[29] and the Kanva Samhita.[30] Although Brahmachari followed the Samaveda,[31] his children accepted the Yajurveda.

Having left behind his wife and home in south-west India, Brahmachari thus created a new family in the North-east. He did not stay with his children, did not eat rice and lived only on fruits. He wore saffron clothes and he was a burly man with a hairy body and a long beard. Hence, he also came to be known as the 'bearded Brahmachari'. He got his three elder sons married to girls from respectable families. Parashuram married Kameswari, the daughter of Laksminath from Sitangshu Sabhapandit's family.

King Gourinath Singha left Rangpur and moved to the Jorhat camp in 1793.[32] After his death in the month of December[33] in 1794,[34] Kamaleswar Singha ascended the throne. When the Kachari king declared war on the Assam

---

[28] Daily rituals.

[29] One of the four Vedas, the main canonical scriptures of the Hindus.

[30] A section of Yajurveda.

[31] One of the four Vedas.

[32] 1716 Sak.

[33] In the original text, the mentioned month is Aghon, which covers November–December. However, December is used here as Gourinath died on 19 December 1794 CE.

[34] 1717 Sak.

king, Haripad Dekaphukan went to battle. Laksminarayan
Brahmachari accompanied them. The Hindustani soldiers
brought by Brahmachari also went with them. Our men
won that hard-fought battle despite suffering major losses.
Burhagohain and others were pleased with Brahmachari's
exploits. Brahmachari wanted to create an accessible
transport link to Bengal. Burhagohain also realized that
the country's welfare was linked with the thoroughfare to
Bengal and Hindustan. He hoped that Brahmachari could
make it happen.

Brahmachari's sons stayed back in Guwahati.
Parashuram resided at Hadira in addition to Guwahati.
Brahmachari is believed to have taken all his sons to
Jorhat once. However, Ranaram always stayed with him.
Brahmachari made the allotment order of Hadirachoki in
Parashuram's name, considering him the most intelligent,
experienced and efficient of the lot. In 1799,[35] with
Burhagohain's nudge, Kamaleswar Singha granted
some Brahmottar[36] land to Brahmachari at Beltola and
Karunabari through a copperplate royal order.

Hadirachoki was the border between Assam and
Bengal. The Duworiya's responsibility was to inform the
king about impending foreign invasions and other such
dangers. He had to collect tolls for taxable items like
ivory tusks, Indian madder and salt from Assam-bound
boats coming from Bengal. He also had to deposit the

---

[35] 1722 Sak.

[36] Rent-free land grant meant for temples and Brahmins.

fixed annual fees at the royal treasury. These were his two principal obligations. Sometimes, searches were conducted on the boats. Brahmachari took charge of that checkpoint by promising to pay 10,000 *narayani taka*[37] along with imported items worth Rs 70,000 per year. The accountant was a young man from Karhal.[38] Other Kakotis[39] were also there. However, Brahmachari felt that the management and bookkeeping were not thorough enough. Hence, he appointed accountants from Kamrup and Bengal. Hariprasad and Satananda from Kamrup, and a few others from Bengal, were appointed for bookkeeping and other tasks. The Duworiya family began to buy westbound exports and eastbound imports and then sell them independently. In a nutshell, they took over almost all businesses in the country. The Duworiya family opened *golas*[40] at Bongalhat, Goalpara, Nagarbera, Guwahati, Darrang and Jorhat towns. These ventures garnered immense profits. The family acquired many soldiers, staff and labourers. Two hundred and forty boats were used to run the business. Brahmachari was a fearless person. Kaliabhomora Borphukan once took offence when Brahmachari told him some unpalatable things about himself and Burhagohain. Babaji had one

---

[37] Currency in circulation in the Koch kingdom.

[38] A place near Nagaon in central Assam.

[39] The class of men in the Ahom court who were responsible for keeping accounts of land, produce and people.

[40] A trade depot of a merchant that also acted as a shop.

necklace containing 108 Shaligram stones. Every day, he also worshipped a Lakshminarayan Shaligram.

Parashuram Barua and his first wife's two sons, Haliram and Jagyaram, were born in 1802[41] and 1804,[42] respectively. Sitanath and Sambhuram were also blessed with children. Brahmachari was delighted with the birth of his grandchildren. After leaving his home and family, Brahmachari had made his new home in a remote part of India. He had acquired a home, children, business and property, and set up a new family line. After some time, an immensely rich Brahmachari went to his heavenly abode on the fourth day in the bright fortnight of the Kati month. For some time before his death, Brahmachari had been the head of the business in name only; Parashuram carried out all the responsibilities. However, now Parashuram became the rightful head. Brahmachari had hoped to hand over the charge to Parashuram and then go on a pilgrimage with Ranaram. Ranaram was very calm and quiet in his childhood. As he always stayed with Brahmachari, Ranaram knew how to look after him. After Brahmachari's demise, Ranaram went on a pilgrimage, taking Brahmachari's ashes with him. He performed his father's *shraddha* and immersed his ashes in the Ganga, Gaya, Kashi, Prayag, Mathura, Brindaban, Haridwar, Setuvandha Rameswar, Jagannath Ksetra and so on. He visited Brahmachari's old home and conveyed the sad news to his wife and other family

---

[41] 1724 Sak.

[42] 1726 Sak.

members. Brahmachari's wife ceased to wear her bangles and began her life as a widow. It was believed that she had cursed that Brahmachari would not be able to continue his lineage. After a long time, Ranaram returned home and married Indrani, the daughter of Bishnuram Hazarika from Athgaon.

The Duworiya family grew richer than it had been in Brahmachari's time. Parashuram assigned specific responsibilities to all his brothers. By then, Patabhiram was no more. Parashuram became the chief Barua. He stayed at either Bongalhat, Guwahati or Jorhat, as required. Shambhuram operated from Bongalhat; hence, he became known as the Barua of Bongalhat. Abhiram stayed in Guwahati, and thus, he came to be known as the Barua of Guwahati. Ranaram stayed in Jorhat and worked from there. He was known as the Barua of Jorhat. Sitaram became a Borbora[43] under the Borphukan of Guwahati. Ranaram was on cordial terms with the king, Burhagohain, and other officials in Jorhat. Laksminath Kothakowa Barua of Bishnudoul was a close confidant of Purnananda Burhagohain. Purnananda requested Ranaram to marry Kothakowa Barua's daughter Sachi, and Ranaram did so. Patoli had been married off to a Mahanta named Gopi some time ago.

---

[43] An official of the Ahom kingdom who commanded a class of subject population.

Kamaleswar Singha died in 1811.[44] King Chandrakanta Singha ascended to the throne. Satram, the son of Kukurachowa[45] Bhut, had evolved as the king's closest friend and was accorded the title of Charingiya Phukan.[46] Animosity brewed between Burhagohain and Satram. Others took the side of one or the other. Swargadeo and the king's mother could not decide what to do. At that moment, Parashuram arrived in Jorhat. The Duworiyas, who were also known as Hatkhowas,[47] were not allowed at the royal court as they did not have designated seating. So, Parashuram became affiliated with the clan of Khound, and Ranaram with the Bez clan. From then on, they could be present at the royal court. Satram asked Parashuram to get some Sikh soldiers from Bongalhat to teach Burhagohain a lesson. However, Laksminath Kothakowa Barua advised Parashuram against it, as Burhagohain was very cunning and influential among the Ahoms. Parashuram also believed that the Duworiya family owed their prosperity to Burhagohain and his father. Therefore, Parashuram asked Satram for some time to gather his soldiers. For that reason and on the charge of not paying the due for Bongalhat, the king ordered one day of jail in the Pilkhana[48] for

---

[44] 1732 Sak.

[45] The incharge of a clan, who looked after royal fowls.

[46] The incharge of a clan who originally belonged to a place called Charing in the Ahom kingdom.

[47] A lessee of a market.

[48] A stable for elephants.

Parashuram. However, Burhagohain saved him from that ordeal.

Soon after, Parashuram returned to Guwahati. In 1811–12,[49] on the order of Burhagohain, Ranaram and Anandaram Gohain went to Kashi to set up a Shiva temple in the name of the king. That temple is still known as the Kamrupi Math. Parashuram followed Brahmachari's system in handling the Duwar[50] and other businesses and accrued immense fortune. After hindering Satram's revolt, Burhagohain sent his men to arrest Badanchandra Borphukan of Guwahati. However, he escaped. Parashuram, by royal decree, sent his men after the Borphukan.

After a while, Parashuram went to his heavenly abode on May 1815.[51] His shraddha ceremony was held on a grand scale. No honorarium was less than Rs 10. The royal palace took umbrage at the grandeur of the ceremony. Parashuram had accumulated a significant volume of wealth during his lifetime. He owned many golas, other businesses and a large number of agricultural farms. At that time, they only drank water carried by a Brahmin. Brahmachari was a vegetarian, so they also did not consume fish or meat. Metal utensils were used for daily cooking. They had many servants and slaves. Shudras[52] could not enter the dining

---

[49] 1734–35 Sak.

[50] Custom checkpoint.

[51] In the original text, the date was the fourth day of the bright fortnight in Bohag, 1738 Sak, which may be converted as 1 May 1815.

[52] Other than Brahmins.

room. Parashuram often rewarded his wives and other relatives with expensive items for anything and everything. He hardly ate due to his ill health despite his immense wealth. Parashuram Barua had married Sudharmana, the daughter of Bishnudev Gosain of Jakhalabandha Satra. He had also married Bhuvaneswari, the daughter of Bishnuram Hazarika of Athgaon and the younger sister of Ranaram's wife, Indrani. However, these wives could not bear him a child. Parashuram Barua had been a very influential man. A foreign tourist who visited this country during his lifetime said there was no one more powerful than Burhagohain in the upper and Parashuram in the lower region. David Scott was the judge and the commissioner of the Rangpur district. He once came to Hadira for a taxation dispute. Scott stayed there for three days but could not meet Parashuram. However, he talked to Haliram, Jagyaram and other junior officers.

Parashuram got Haliram and Jagyaram educated with great care. At that time, people believed that a person who learnt non-Hindu[53] languages was not eligible to offer *pinda*[54] and perform *tarpan*[55] for his ancestors. Traditionally, the eldest son offers pinda. Therefore, Haliram was taught only the Sanskrit language. Jagyaram was allowed to learn

---

[53] *Jabonik*, which was used to describe Greek or Mohammedan population.

[54] Ritualistic offering to ancestors prepared from cooked rice mixed with ghee and black sesame seeds in Hindu rites.

[55] Offerings made to parents and ancestors.

both Sanskrit and Persian, an Islamic language. Both excelled in their education.

Haliram was appointed as the Duworiya Barua after the demise of Parashuram Barua. He was fourteen years old at that time. Ranaram became their guardian, working with the earlier team. Sambhuram, Abhiram and Sitaram had already separated from the joint family. Only Ranaram lived with the family.

In 1816,[56] Badanchandra Borphukan went to Myanmar and brought the Burmese army to Jorhat in the upper region. People fled to different places. Purnananda Burhagohain died, after which Badanchandra became the Phukan.[57] After a while, the Burmese army returned to their own country after declaring Chandrakanta Singha as the king. Badan was beheaded. Purnananda's son, Ruchinath, along with other people, dethroned Chandrakanta Singha. They made Purandar Singha the new king. After learning about this development, the Burmese king sent his army in 1821.[58] Purandar Singha fled westwards, and Chandrakanta Singha was returned his kingship. After a while, the Burmese king sent a troop to assess the situation on the ground. King Chandrakanta mistook it for an invasion and sent his men to stop them. After defeating our army, the Burmese military entered the capital. The king fled, as he could not

---

[56] In the original text, the year 1739 Sak is mentioned too.

[57] A high-ranking official in the Ahom court.

[58] 1740 Sak.

stop the Burmese invasion. There was chaos everywhere, with people running away to different places.

The volatile situation in the country prompted Haliram to shift his base to Hadira from the Guwahati camp. He left behind many of his belongings in Guwahati. Many boats and properties got lost. King Chandrakanta went further west.

Meanwhile, the Burmese reached Hadira. Duworiya's battalion consisting of Sikhs and others fought with the Burmese forces. In the ensuing battle, Chaitanya Singh Subadar and other soldiers were killed.

Haliram demonstrated outstanding bravery in this battle. After losing his soldiers, he jumped into his own boat but was pierced in the neck by a musket bayonet that was on the boat. He managed to pull it out and bandaged his neck using fabric from his turban. After that, he navigated his boat downstream and reached Jogighopa.

Women from his family rode on a boat with as many belongings as they could. Their servants and others were also on board. Meanwhile, after defeating our army, the Burmese charged towards these boats. The ladies' boat carried Haliram's mother and his two stepmothers, Jagyaram, Ranaram, his seniormost wife, and their two children, Bijoyram and Jagyeswari. It also carried Sarbeswari, the sister of Parashuram's youngest wife. While trying to sail, the sailors could not move the boat. It got stuck in the shallow water, even after the sailors tried their best. Meanwhile, Haliram's mother prayed earnestly to the Brahmaputra by offering the river one of the gold rings she was wearing, along with betel nuts and leaves. Suddenly, the boat moved into deep water, and they then sailed down to Jogighopa. Many of their properties were left behind at Hadira and were lost. At Goalpara, they had a *kuth*[59] made for their gola. That structure was built in Parashuram Barua's time. The port adjacent to the present court is still known as the Kuthi port. After leaving instructions for the gola's manager and other officials about their duties, Haliram and the others went to Silamari in the district of Rangpur after a few days. Our king, Burhagohain, other officials, and many refugees were already taking refuge there. Kalikanta Saha and Ramakanta Saha, who belonged to the Sau[60] or Suri[61] caste, lived there. They had a gola at Jogighopa and had trade relations with the Duworiya family. That's why Kalikanta and Ramakanta Saha took great care of this family. Locals got annoyed as our refugees plucked tamarinds from their orchards. Shouting, 'Hey sister, the Assam people are plucking tamarind from the trees!' they charged towards the refugees. After arranging for some soldiers, King Chandrakanta went up to the east. The British government had already stationed Lieutenant Davidson at Goalpara to secure the border.

Meanwhile, after learning about the situation in Assam from Scott sahab, the British government planned to come here. Haliram and the others thought staying put at Silamari

---

[59] A concrete structure.

[60] A Bengali Hindu caste.

[61] A Bengali Hindu caste.

would be useless. They decided to wait and watch. For now, they would go for a Gangasnan.[62] Thus, all of them went to Murshidabad for the ritual bath. *Keyans* or Marwaris had shops in Guwahati and Goalpara, and had trade relations with the Duworiya family. A few of those Marwaris also had golas and acquaintances at Murshidabad. Through them, the Duworiyas also knew the family of the renowned Jagat Seth of Murshidabad. The Duworiyas, too, had business transactions with them. Therefore, they did not face any difficulty there. During an eclipse, Haliram, Jagyaram, their mothers and two stepmothers were initiated by a Dandi Swami[63] at the Ganga riverside. They made a ceremonial gift of gold to the Dandi Swami. After staying on the shore of the Ganga for a while, they returned to Chandariya at Goalpara and resumed their gola business. Meanwhile, Sambhuram and Abhiram constructed separate houses and shifted there. Kushadev Adhikari Gosain from Ahatguri of Majuli fled to Goalpara and stayed there. Haliram married Kushadev's eldest daughter, Prasuti. Just as the final offering at the *hom*[64] was being made on the wedding night, a fire suddenly broke out in the interior part of their house, damaging it along with many household items. Chaudolas[65] and Bengali courtesan singers had not been

---

[62] Hindu ritualistic bathing in the Ganga.

[63] Dandi Swami is a sect of Indian saints who believe Sankaracharyas are chosen from among them.

[64] A ritual wherein offerings are made into a consecrated fire.

[65] A palanquin born by four people.

arranged for at this wedding. For this, Haliram expressed his slight annoyance to Ranaram, as he was the guardian till then. After a while, Jagyaram married the sister of Laksminath of the Bezbarua clan. That wedding rectified all the shortcomings of the earlier one. This marriage was celebrated with great pomp. Goalpara had not seen such a grand marriage till then. The elders of Goalpara and Chandaria still talk about this wedding. Chandradhar Ray, Giridhar Ray, Jayadhar Ray, Chandiprasad Ray, Ramprasad Ghosh and others worked for the Duworiya family as *gomastas*[66] in their business and household. They also managed everything that involved writing. Meanwhile, Scott entered Assam with his army and chased away the Burmese. He gained a lot of information about Assam from the Duworiya family and also received massive help. After conquering the country, Scott advised the Assamese people, who had taken refuge at Jogighopa and Pagalatek in Goalpara, to return to their own country.

Scott had known Haliram and Jagyaram for a long time. They wanted to return to Guwahati; the sahab advised them the same. After the death of his first wife, Jagyaram married Barada, the eldest daughter of Kushachandra Gosain of Diphalu Satra. After constructing a house at Bharalumukh, they came to live there in 1826.[67] Just before that, Haliram and Jagyaram had decided to live separately. They agreed to share Ranaram, their mother and the Gopal

---

[66] A steward, agent or subordinate officer of a merchant.

[67] 1748 Sak.

idol. The middle stepmother would stay with Jagyaram, and the youngest one would be with Haliram. All their estates would remain common property. Ranaram would get maintenance from both brothers. Ranaram was an upright man. He did not like to be involved in the mess of properties. So, he was not sad to be relieved of his role as the head and felt content with the arrangement. At Guwahati, Ranaram lived in the east, Haliram in the centre and Jagyaram to the west of the same campus. Later, four government roads were constructed around their campus. Sitaram lived in the north of the northern road. Sambhuram and Abhiram remained at Goalpara. Scott sahab took Haliram with him on his journey to the east; Haliram eventually became the sahab's chief assistant. After staying in Guwahati for some time, Jagyaram left for Calcutta, where he attended the preaching of the renowned Rammohan Roy. Roy, a stalwart of India, was the head preacher of the sacred Brahmo religion. Jagyaram was among the first few with whom Roy performed the Brahmopasana.[68]

As chief assistant to Scott, Haliram toured Assam with him. He made the first settlement[69] of Darrang and Nagaon. People in Nagaon still reminisce about this settlement. While in Guwahati, King Chandrakanta Singha appointed Haliram as the Dhekial Phukan[70] and

---

[68] Worship of the Infinite Brahma.

[69] Land revenue settlement carried out as part of the English East India Company's early administrative reforms in Assam.

[70] The chief of the Dhekial clan.

Jagyaram as the Khargharia Phukan.[71] Scott, the chief
agent of the government at that period, put the seal on
these appointments.

When the province's upper and lower regions were
rechristened as the junior and senior divisions, Haliram
Phukan remained in the senior, i.e., lower division. As the
sheristadar,[72] Haliram was entrusted specifically with the
settlement of Kamrup. Major White,[73] a British officer
was posted in Kamrup at that time. After an argument
over a trivial matter with White sahab, Haliram resigned.
Learning about this dispute, Scott blamed Major White.
Haliram Dhekial Phukan usually went to the court in a
covered palanquin. Others got down from the palanquin
in front of Scott sahab. They also put aside their *borjapis*[74]
in front of him. However, Haliram did none of this to
show respect to Scott sahab. That is why sahab respected
him. A civilized person respects another with self-respect.
He took Haliram's advice in almost every matter. During
the Nagaon settlement, Haliram married Tilottama or
Kalyani, the daughter of Lavachandra Gosain, the head of
Deephalu Satra.

---

[71] The official is the incharge of the royal arms and ammunition
store in the Ahom kingdom.

[72] The supervisor of the collectorate.

[73] Major Adam White of the Bengal Native Infantry was the
political agent of the East India Company in Upper Assam during
1832–39.

[74] A large hat made of bamboo.

After their return to Guwahati, Haliram Phukan's wife, Prasuti Devi, gave birth to a girl who died soon after. In 1828,[75] Jagyaram Phukan had a baby boy named Durgaram. On a Tuesday, 22 September, 1829,[76] Haliram had a boy with his wife, Prasuti Devi. Born under the Pushya star and Cancer zodiac, the boy had two names: Ananda Ram as the official name and Hemakantha as the concealed name.[77] In the Kati[78] month of the same year, Kalyani Devi delivered Haliram's daughter. Her official name was Tuloshi, and her concealed name was Tarini. Both Ananda Ram and Tuloshi became the apples of their parents' eyes. The Barua of Kamrup's Barnagar Pargana brought a girl named Juti to be Ananda Ram's nanny. During that period, Scott sahab, stationed in Cherrapunjee, subdued the local Khasis.

Earlier, while he was still in Goalpara, Haliram went on a pilgrimage to the Ganga, Gaya, Kashi, Prayag and so on. He was a renowned philanthropist, especially donating a lot during the pilgrimage. He accomplished his duties admirably in every holy place he visited. A great scholar

---

[75] 1750 Sak.

[76] 7 Ahin, 1751 Sak is equivalent to 22 September 1829 in the Gregorian calendar. See Samuel Smith and Co, The Bengal Almanac for the year 1829 with a companion and appendix (Calcutta: Bengal Hurkaru and Chronicle Press), p. xix.

[77] In Assam, a Hindu baby receives two names during the naming ceremony. Of these, the *gupta* or the concealed name is used only for religious purposes and is not publicly shared.

[78] October–November.

of Sanskrit and Tantra texts,[79] there was no sacred place
where he did not earn respect from the local scholars. Thus,
he spent a great deal on donations and charity. The *pandas*[80]
from those shrines still recall Haliram Dhekial Phukan as
the most prominent pilgrim from Assam.

Jagyaram studied English and other scriptures upon
visiting Calcutta. As Rammohan Roy was a Brahmo
and Jagyaram was now his student, a rumour spread that
Jagyaram had also become a Brahmo.[81] At that time, the term
Brahmo was not very prevalent—they were called Christians
instead. Learning about his brother's conversion, Haliram
wanted to go to Calcutta to bring back Jagyaram. At that
point, Haliram had a dispute with White sahab. According
to hearsay, Haliram had vowed not to return to this country
until he could officiate in a capacity similar to Major White.

White sahab was an irascible man. He knew from
others that Haliram was a man with an ego. As he could not
differentiate between ego and honour, Major White became
annoyed with Haliram. One day, he mistreated Haliram in
court. Haliram responded equally. Soon after, Haliram went
to Calcutta after resigning, journeying through Dhaka and the
Sundarbans. However, Jagyaram returned via Murshidabad.
He brought an English teacher with him. While returning,

---

[79] A scripture of religious worship and practices.

[80] A Brahman priest acting as a guide to pilgrims at holy places.

[81] A follower of Brahmoism, a socio-religious movement founded
by Raja Rammohan Roy in colonial Bengal.

after settling the outstanding accounts with Jagat Seth, he
brought valuable ornaments such as Sarpesh, Kalgi and so
on.[82] After returning home, Jagyaram remained in Guwahati
for some time. Haliram visited Calcutta before going to
Shreekshetra.[83] During his visit, he generously donated a
large sum of money to charity. While stationed in Silamari,
King Chandrakanta had taken a loan from the Duworiyas by
mortgaging a gold urn to pay his sepoys. Despite objections
from others, Haliram offered that urn to Lord Jagannath,
which received immense praise. Even today, Gadadhar
Panda tries to attract Assamese pilgrims in the name of
Haliram Dhekial Phukan. From Sreekshetra, Haliram
returned to Calcutta. At that time, people knew little about
Assam and Kamrup Kamakhya. It was often regarded as the
land of witches and yoginis.[84] Haliram compiled a Sanskrit
text, *Kamakhya Yatra Paddhati*, drawing from Yoginitantra,[85]
Kalikapurana[86] and other texts. He documented every
detail of the sacred visit to Kamakhya and other shrines in
Kamrup, including their worship practices. He also authored
a Bengali book, *Asam Buranji*, in which he discussed various

---

[82] Sarpesh and Kalki are ornaments worn on the turban.

[83] Puri in the Indian state of Odissa.

[84] Female practitioner of yogas and tantras.

[85] A medieval Tantric text belonging to the sixteenth to seventeenth
century.

[86] A Hindu religious text and is one of the minor Puranas
(*Upapurana*) believed to have been written between the ninth and
eleventh centuries.

aspects of the country and the history of its kings. In 1830,[87] these two books were printed at the Samachar Chandrika Press in Calcutta and distributed free of cost. Haliram became acquainted with eminent rajas and other notable personalities and also joined the Dharmasabha[88]society as a member. Haliram garnered considerable attention in Calcutta. One local newspaper, coining a pun with his name, wrote, 'A Mus-Haliram Dhenki has arrived in Calcutta.'[89] Another one played a pun on Haliram's nature of getting involved in various discourses:[90] 'One Dhenki has arrived here from Kamrup Kamakhya,[91] riding on a "dhenki tree"[92] and is making a lot of noise.' Haliram enjoyed these jokes thoroughly. The people of Calcutta presumed him to be the king of Assam. After staying in Calcutta for some time, Haliram returned to Guwahati.

After the demise of Scott sahab at Cherrapunji, Cracroft was appointed as commissioner. Our people pronounced his name as 'Kerikerapot'. This British man was aware

---

[87] 1753 Sak.

[88] Dharma Sabha was an association founded by Radhakanta Deb.

[89] In Bengali language, mushal means a part of a dhenki, a pedal used for pounding rice.

[90] The persona of Haliram was likened to Narad, the Hindu sage renowned in Assamese and Bengali folk culture for his involvement in debates, often causing trouble, and his unique mode of transport, the 'dhenki'.

[91] Assam was mostly known as Kamrup Kamakhya in Bengal.

[92] In Bengali, dhenki also means an edible fern.

of Haliram's efficiency. Haliram was appointed assistant magistrate in Guwahati after the government sanctioned the post. His monthly salary was Rs 230.

Ranaram's daughter, Jagyeswari, married Dhirchandra Goswami of Diphalu Satra. Quite a few children born to Ranaram's first wife died shortly after birth. Only two sons, Bijayram and Gangaram, and a daughter named Lileshi survived. Jagyeswari was the only child of his second wife. Haliram introduced the ritual of worshipping and fasting for Goddess Mangal Chandi[93] from Kashi. It is said that observing this fast helps with conception. Jagyeswari's mother observed the fast for one year, after which she gave birth to a son. She endured a lot during childbirth, but a British doctor from Guwahati performed a surgery that saved her life.

Sitaram filed a case in court, demanding a sum of Rs 9,72,000 as his share of the property. The case was settled out of court. Jagyaram Phukan, after being appointed as a police superintendent, went to Jorhat, with Bijayram accompanying him.

Haliram had a weak disposition and suffered from *vata* imbalance[94] from time to time. In the monsoon of 1831,[95] Haliram, along with his seniormost wife and son Ananda

---

[93] A manifestation of Goddess Chandi.

[94] In Ayurveda, vata governs the movements in the body, activities of the nervous system. Increase of Vata *implies the imbalance of air and space elements in the body.*

[95] 1754 Sak.

Ram, went to the Umananda hill and resided there. From there, he would travel to the court for his duties. He was performing the Mahamrityunjaya Shiva puja[96] in the Umananda temple. On the morning of the thirteenth day of the dark fortnight of the Saon month, he woke up and washed himself and went to bed again as he was feeling unwell. He used to take opium regularly for good health and also consumed prescribed medicine every morning. Before going to bed, Haliram ordered his Brahmin aide, Ramdutta, to wake him up after preparing the medication. Ramdutta called Haliram after preparing the medicine but received no answer. After some time, he tried again but still got no response. When he touched Haliram, he realized that Haliram had gone cold and was no longer breathing. Fearing the worst, Ramdutta informed everyone, and they realized that Haliram was no more. A lot of people gathered after receiving the news. He was cremated a little below the Umananda temple, towards the east. The Mahamrityunjaya worship could not be completed. His family returned to their Guwahati home, where Dhekial Phukan's Adya Shraddha[97] ceremony was performed on a grand scale. At the Sukreswar temple, Brahmins were given their due honorariums.

---

[96] This worship is meant for longevity, good health and preventing an untimely death.

[97] A funeral rite or ceremony performed in honour of the departed spirits of dead relatives.

Haliram Phukan was an exceptionally prominent person in this country. He was extremely proficient in Bengali and Sanskrit languages and could speak Sanskrit as fluently as his mother tongue. A philanthropist at heart, he donated generously to various causes. Notably, he provided the urn that adorns the top of the Kamakhya temple. He also made substantial donations to temples such as Umananda, Hayagriv-Madhav, Ugratara, among other places. He had deep knowledge of Tantric[98] and Tantra texts and was deeply devoted to gods and Brahmins. He regularly performed puja, *hom*, Shanti[99] and Swastayan.[100] He celebrated Basanti Puja,[101] Siddha Ganesh Puja,[102] Annapurna Puja[103] and other pujas extravagantly.

In addition to his religious contributions, Haliram helped others to the best of his ability. However, he could not tolerate disrespect. He never sacrificed his own dignity to show respect to others, and he strongly disliked it when others did so. Once, an Ahom gentleman came to meet him. Haliram showed him due respect and offered him a seat, and they talked. While leaving, that gentleman

---

[98] A practitioner of Tantra texts.

[99] A ritual performed to get relief from ailment, snake bite, etc.

[100] A ritual performed to obtain prosperity and discard evil.

[101] Worship of Goddess Durga held in the month of Chot, i.e., March–April.

[102] Siddha Ganesh is one form of Lord Ganesha.

[103] A manifestation of Parvati and is known as the Hindu Goddess of food and nourishment.

approached Haliram, kneeled down and said something to him. Haliram disapproved of that gesture.

He acted judiciously in every official position he held. Even when unwell, he never abandoned his daily rituals. His aide would offer him water or a flower, he would then recite chants, after which the aide offered the water or flower to the nearby idol, yantra[104] or Shaligram. Nomal and Hemakantha, members of the royal physician family, used to stay with him and administered his medication. At the time, his mother and maternal grandfather were still alive.

Haliram was a very hard-working and diligent man. Despite his busy schedule during the day, he performed a brief morning worship but dedicated more time to an elaborate evening worship. He was an influential figure and an expert in administration. Haliram did not look down on Bengalis or Hindustanis as outcasts; instead, he tried to settle them in this country by giving them job opportunities. He was interested in vocal and instrumental music too. At his home, music concerts were often organized during celebrations or otherwise. They had a gorgeous drawing room[105] full of expensive items in an outhouse.[106] A fire destroyed this room, and many things were lost. The

---

[104] In Tantric Hinduism and Tantric Buddhism, Yantra refers to a linear diagram used as a support for rituals.

[105] Boithakkhana.

[106] The original word was Chauwari. Chaubari means a penthouse, private room, a porch, etc., in Hindi and Urdu.

foundation of that house remained intact until just a few years ago. Each year, Haliram and his family celebrated festivals such as Holi, Janmastami,[107] Ganesh Puja and more. In addition to these, during the month of Kati, a *havishya*-observing[108] Brahmin would light a sky lantern and offer basil leaves to the gods every day. In Magh, a Brahmin would read the Gita every day. During Durga Puja, a small pitcher was placed[109] and a Chandipath[110] was held. In the month of Puh,[111] khichiri[112] was offered to the family deity and Brahmins. Ceremonial feasts for Brahmins were organized in Magh, and Satyanarayan Puja[113] and offering of basil leaves[114] were held every month. Lakshmi worship was celebrated on the holy nights of Kojagar[115] and Deepavali.[116] Apart from these, other Swastayan ceremonies were regularly held. Some of these

---

[107] Occasion of the birthday of Shreekrishna.

[108] A single boiled vegetarian meal without oil, consumed during a fast.

[109] Ceremonial placing of a pitcher full of holy water on the altar making the commencement of worship.

[110] Recital of a Hindu scriptural book.

[111] December–January.

[112] A food prepared by boiling rice and dal together with spices and fat.

[113] A religious ritual worship of the Hindu god Vishnu.

[114] The original text mentions *tuloshi daan*.

[115] The full moon night in the month of Ahin-Kati.

[116] The festival of illumination.

celebrations were organized jointly by both households, while others were independent events.

Beltola, Karunabari, Phulara, Kharadhara, Tholabari, Haripur and Borhata estates were shared properties of both households, along with another estate at Gog. These estates were managed by *gomastas* and *mukhtars*.[117] The overall incharge was Chandradhar Ray. Later, a man from Bikrampur named Ramchandra Biswas was appointed as the mukhtar from the elder's side. Both households had separate golas in Guwahati and a joint gola in Darrang. They had countless servants and maids at their mansions. Apart from them, they had other servants, bonded and hired labourers, working in the estates. Rice, gram and other items were brought in daily from the farms. These were transported in carts drawn by buffaloes, bulls and horses. Items from individual farms were stored in individual granaries, whereas things from collective farms went to their individual granaries after dividing them. The settlement of land share and taxes for the tenant farmers of the farms were fixed. At the time of Haliram's death, such was the arrangement between the two households.

Jagyaram Phukan had a son in 1831[118] at Jorhat. He was named Balaram. After a while, when Purandar Singha was made the tributary king of Upper Assam, Jagyaram returned to Guwahati from Jorhat and was appointed as

---

[117] A rent collector; an agent or employee of a merchant or a company.

[118] 1753 Sak.

the Sadar Amin.[119] Ranaram, who was officiating in the panchayat in Darrang, returned to Guwahati shortly before Haliram's death. King Purandar Singha, compelled to go to Upper Assam, decided to rule the region in the erstwhile system. He appointed Haliram's son Ananda Ram as the new Dhekial Phukan. Jagyaram Phukan remained the Khargharia Phukan. As Ananda Ram was a minor and Jagyaram had other obligations, with a royal decree, Ranaram went to Jorhat to officiate for both posts. Nagaon and Darrang were separated into different districts, and the senior division was abolished in 1830.

Upon returning home, Jagyaram Phukan began managing the farms of both households and worked to recover loans from borrowers, handling all matters efficiently. Shortly thereafter, Ranaram's son Bijayram died. Several Choudhurys, Patwaris,[120] and other tenants from their estates stayed at camps within the Phukan campus, relying on their support. Many other dependants also lived on the campus.

---

119 A commissioner or arbitrator, a native civil judge.

120 An official who keeps records regarding the ownership of land.

Part I

Part I

Chapter 1

On 22 September 1829,[121] Ananda Ram Phookan was born under the zodiac sign of Cancer. His birth brought immense joy to his family, and his father, Haliram, spared no expense on donations and offerings. Ananda Ram was showered with love and affection, though little is remembered about his childhood antics. As a toddler, he did not behave like other children, even when his parents showed affection to other kids. On one occasion, his mother had to breastfeed his cousin Gangaram when the latter's mother was experiencing breast pain, yet Ananda Ram did not throw a tantrum.

Overall, Ananda Ram was a chubby and healthy child. At times, he would be cross, but he always played joyfully with his sister and other boys. However, he rarely approached Haliram when he was home, as he was afraid of his father. Despite this, he was not afraid of interacting with others. Ranaram Barua loved him dearly, and Ananda Ram would often reach up to touch his bald head while

---

[121] In the original text, it is the seventh Ahin in 1751 Sak, which can be converted as 22 September 1829 CE.

sitting on his lap. Tragically, Ananda Ram was only three years old when his father passed away. Though he could not fully comprehend the loss, he cried several times upon seeing others in sorrow. As he grew, he cherished his father's memory like a dream. His *Churakaran*[122] ceremony had been performed while his father was still alive.

After his formal initiation into learning[123] at the age of five, Ananda Ram began his education under the guidance of various teachers. One of them was Jashodhar from Umananda. After a while, he, along with his cousin Durgaram, learnt Sanskrit grammar, including *Karika Ratnamala* and *Mugdhavodha*, as well as conjugation. Gangaram, Ranaram's son, and Balaram, Jagyaram's youngest son, also joined in learning to read and write in Bengali. However, Ananda Ram's progress was not as promising as it could have been. Jagyaram was very involved in their education. In 1835, an English school and a Bengali school were established with the support of the government and the public. Jagyaram provided both financial support and enthusiasm for the project, as he was the most notable local figure and the only resident fluent in English. Ananda Ram and Durgaram were enrolled in the English school in 1837.

That year, Ranaram returned from Jorhat, where his youngest wife had given birth to a son named Gunabhiram.

---

[122] The first haircut or shaving of the head of a male child, a Hindu ritual.

[123] Vidyarambha.

Ananda Ram was thrilled to see his uncle after such a long time. However, Ananda Ram's mother was not pleased with Jagyaram following a disagreement and wished to move to one of their estates. Ranaram advised against this, as it would disrupt Ananda Ram's education. Tragically, Ranaram passed away in May 1838.[124]

Shortly after, in July, Jagyaram fell ill with a fever and moved to Captain Matthie's bungalow for treatment and fresh air. When his condition worsened, he was brought back home, where he passed away that month.[125]

Jagyaram was a serious man, skilled in several languages including Sanskrit, Bengali, English, Persian, Arabic, Bhutanese and Urdu. Trained by Raja Rammohan Roy, he adopted a progressive and refined approach towards religion and society. He treated the British as his equals and had close friendships with Captain Jenkins,[126] the commissioner, and Captain James Matthie, the deputy commissioner. Before he passed away, Jagyaram asked Captain Matthie to take care of his house and children. He was briefly involved in elephant trading and even travelled

---

[124] In the Assamese text, it was the fourth day of the bright fortnight of the month of Jeth in 1760 Sak, which can be converted as 27 May 1838 CE.

[125] In the original text, the date is the second day of the bright fortnight of Saon, 1760 Sak, which can be converted as 23 July 1838 CE.

[126] Francis Jenkins.

to Mymensingh.[127] There, he engaged in debates on various topics for days with a zamindar named Nabababu. At one point, he travelled to Dhaka for medical treatment. After Jagyaram's death, his family was left without a guardian. Captain Matthie took them under his wing, overseeing their education and upbringing, while the staff managed the estates, businesses and annual rituals.

Ananda Ram was a dedicated student who never missed a day of school. He occasionally visited Matthie sahab, Jenkins sahab and Wilms sahab, who were close to the local community and deeply committed to its welfare. Their homes were always open and they generously provided students with books, papers, money and other necessities. The students had access to their elephants, horses, boats, buggies and gardens, and often went on outings to the park. Matthie sahab and Jenkins sahab organized these fun activities during pujas and other festivals. They even participated in the boys' games, encouraging them to run, wrestle or climb trees for prizes. They created an environment that supported the physical, mental and moral development of the students. Ananda Ram flourished under their guidance and care.

Every day, Ananda Ram would wake up early, prepare for his lessons, bathe at home or in the Bharalu or Brahmaputra River and then head to school after having a quick breakfast. He had been riding horses and buggies since he was a young child. When he turned eleven, Durgaram performed his

---

[127] Now in Bangladesh.

sacred thread ceremony; Durgaram's own ceremony had already been performed by Krishnadev from the Teokiya Adhyapak clan. Ananda Ram's stepsister Tuloshi married Raghudev Goswami, the eldest son of Chandrakanta Adhikari of Jakhalabandha Satra. The groom's party camped on the Brahmaputra riverside and brought their palanquins and borjapis inside the Phukan campus, which caused some annoyance on our side. However, no complaints were made, as one should not find fault with guests. Jogeswar Goswami of North Guwahati sent a team to perform a farce using bows and arrows during the wedding.

After his sacred thread ceremony, Ananda Ram learnt to perform the Sandhya[128] thrice a day, except on special occasions like the twelfth day of a fortnight, a shraddha ceremony or Sankranti.[129] He preferred a thick and spotless sacred thread. Ananda Ram was a stickler for daily rituals and cleanliness. He enjoyed playing games like Choupat[130] and cards. He also played other games such as Bhotaguti,[131] Hoi Gudu,[132] Photikolai,[133] Ghila[134] and Latim,[135] though

---

[128] Prayer offered at morning, noon or evening.

[129] These rituals are forbidden on these particular days.

[130] A game of dice.

[131] A traditional game played with a wooden ball and a stick.

[132] A popular traditional game much like kabaddi.

[133] A traditional game.

[134] A game of two groups trying to put the *ghila* or the dice in a hole.

[135] A spinning top.

he never got addicted. During Holi, like other boys, he would even throw colours at passers-by. Once, while playing Choupat with his friends Durgaram, Haranath and others, Haranath lost a game and ran away, babbling a nonsensical rhyme, which left Ananda Ram in stitches.

Many people still remembered the calamities they endured during the Burmese invasion. Ananda Ram, Durgaram, Balaram, Gangaram and their other friends occasionally fought mock war with bamboo, *ikora*[136] or *khagari*[137] bows and arrows, with one team role-playing the Burmese and the other, the British. They also enjoyed swimming in the river and picnicking on the riverbank during the winter. A five-day worship took place during Holi celebrations, and the entire family participated with great enthusiasm. This festival was filled with music, dance, concerts and fireworks, attracting both Marwaris and other gentlemen to join in the festivities, whether during the day or at night. Ananda Ram took part in the celebrations and thoroughly enjoyed the time spent with his family and guests. He was always polite to visitors and fascinated by folktales and stories from the past, a passion that began when he was a small child.

Mahodar Khangia Barua worked as a *nazir*[138] at the collectorate in Guwahati and assisted Scott sahab during the invasion of Assam. As an envoy of King Chandrakanta,

---

[136] A type of reed.

[137] Elephant grass.

[138] A bailiff.

he once travelled to Calcutta to deliver a message to the government. Mahodar's nephew, Madhavram, married Ranaram's daughter, Lileshi, while his other nephew, Gobindaram, married Sitaram's daughter, Nareswari. Mahodar's second son, Parashuram, was born in the same month as Ananda Ram, and they both lived in Panbazar. Parashuram, who lost his father at a young age, attended school with Matthie's support and became best friends with Ananda Ram. They often visited each other's homes.

Ananda Ram visited Kamakhya during Durga Puja and frequently went to temples such as Umananda, Aswaklanta and Bashishtha. However, he viewed these places purely as sacred sites for worship and nothing more. Despite being more intelligent than his peers, Ananda Ram was not yet progressive or reformed in his beliefs.

At a low price, Ananda Ram bought land, including agricultural property, in Ramshaha Pargana from a previous owner named Driver sahab.[139] This estate, located near Dopdar, had several ancient ponds. Over time, many tenants settled there.

Krishnaram Nyaybagish Bhattacharjya, a scholar from Santipur in Nadia, was invited by King Rudra Singha to Assam. The succeeding king, Siva Singha, became his disciple. Many people followed him, and he was granted substantial land to settle on Nilachal Hill in Guwahati. Living on a hill, he was known as Parbatiya Gosain, meaning 'Gosain from the hill'. His household was divided into three

---

[139] H. Driver, who later became a colleague of Ananda Ram.

families: the eldest, middle and youngest. The eldest family
had several children, including Kalidas Bhattacharjya, who
was intelligent and charismatic. Haliram, his first wife and
Jagyeswar were disciples of Dandi Swami, while Haliram's
other wives were disciples of other respected families.
However, they did not have a family guru. In those times,
the Parbatiya Gosain household was the most revered.
After much deliberation with Kalidas Bhattacharjya,
Ananda Ram became his disciple on September 1841,[140]
and observed puja with great devotion. Meanwhile,
Durgaram became a disciple of Umakanta from the
youngest Bhattacharjya family.

The previous year, Matthie sahab and Jenkins sahab
had helped a few boys from Guwahati, named Kirtikanta,
Madhavchandra, Holiram and Chandramal, to study in
Calcutta. Ananda Ram was a diligent and enthusiastic
student who impressed his teachers, Singer and
Robinson,[141] and won prizes every year. Jenkins, Matthie
and other British officers were impressed by Ananda
Ram's and Durgaram's abilities and good behaviour and
encouraged them to pursue their studies in Calcutta.
However, their mother, grandmother and other relatives
were against this decision. At that time, travelling to
Calcutta was not as easy as it is now, and sailing was the

---

[140] In the original text the date is the eighth day of the month of Ahin
of 1763 Sak, which may be converted to 22 September 1841 CE.

[141] A. Singer was the first Headmaster of the school, and William
Robinson followed him as Headmaster.

only option, which was fraught with thieves and robbers. Calcutta's climate was also considered unhealthy, and the water was saline, causing frequent illness. In the past, Bengalis rarely visited Assam, and these communities had little awareness of each other. Ananda Ram and Durgaram were too young to handle the challenges of living in a foreign place, which worried their mothers. Ananda Ram was so upset by their reluctance that he refused to eat for a while. The two sahabs sent almost an order through their mukhtar for sending the boys to Calcutta. Their mothers had no other option but to reluctantly agree to this proposal.

Matthie and Jenkins used to obtain their necessities from Calcutta through their personal boats. Travelling was far more challenging than it is today. Matthie sahab provided one of his cargo boats, which could carry up to 600 *maunds*,[142] for the boys' journey. Durgaram brought a Brahmin cook named Ramdev from Sila and three house-born servants[143] named Phalaram, Binanda and Anadar. Ananda Ram's companions were Shreedhar, a Brahmin cook from Borbhag, *bharali*[144] Misir, mukhtar Ramchandra Biswas and a servant. They embarked on their journey on an auspicious day during the monsoon season of 1841. They

---

[142] A unit of weight used in India, having a value of approximately 82 pounds or 40 kilogrammes.

[143] They were born in the Phukan house as their parents were employed in the latter's house.

[144] Bharali means the in charge of a store or bharal, e.g., granary.

made vows to offer a white buffalo to Goddess Kamakhya and other offerings to various gods for a safe return after a successful trip. They also promised to perform Shanti-Swastayan worship. Matthie sent his peon with them and provided introductions for Ananadaram and Durgaram to various companies and influential individuals in Calcutta, such as Calvin Company, Canter Company, Kerogson Company, Mouat,[145] Halliday[146] and Beckett.[147] They also made arrangements to receive the necessary funds from these companies. Marwari gola owners who had trade relations with the Phukan family, such as Budhsing, Sobhachand, Himmatsing, Ratanchand, Mayasing and others, wrote to their Calcutta golas to introduce Ananda Ram and Durgaram.

The boat journey towards the west commenced, and the passengers' mood lifted as they progressed. Ramchandra Biswas, hailing from Bikrampur in the Dhaka district, pointed out the various places along the way, delighting the passengers. The two cousins were particularly impressed by the kuth in Goalpara, constructed by Parashuram. The boat then made its way through Sirajganj, Dhaka and the

[145] Dr F.J. Mouat was a professor of chemistry and materia medica at Calcutta Medical College. He was also a member of the Council of Education, Bengal government.

[146] Frederick James Halliday was a British civil servant and the first Lieutenant-Governor of Bengal.

[147] Charles Beckett Greenlaw, coroner of Calcutta and secretary, Bengal, played a key role in introducing steam communication in India.

Sundarbans, eventually reaching Calcutta after twenty-five days. The passengers were overjoyed upon arriving in Calcutta, admiring the ships, stunning buildings, bustling streets, busy ports and the large crowds. Their spirits lifted even more after meeting the individuals who had received their introduction letters. The passengers rented a house in Kalutola, Calcutta, and settled in.

In Calcutta, the Hindu College was established with contributions from the city's affluent citizens and the government. Hindu boys attended the school, where they learned English and Bengali for a monthly fee of Rs 5. The school was managed by a committee of wealthy and knowledgeable local and international members, with Rasamay Dutta,[148] a native of Calcutta, serving as secretary and Hare[149] as the visitor. During this period, Bengal's education system was overseen by the Council of Education, with various native and English gentlemen serving as members. Jenkins and Matthie wrote to these committees to introduce Ananda Ram and Durgaram. Both Phukans were encouraged by the committee members. The boys were admitted to the third class of the junior department at Hindu College, having previously been in the first class at

---

[148] Rasamay Dutta, a philanthropist, was the co-founder of the Hindu School.

[149] David Hare was a Scottish watchmaker and philanthropist in Calcutta.

Guwahati School.[150] Upon their arrival in Calcutta, Ananda Ram and Durgaram could already communicate in English with Europeans and even write letters in the language to some extent. After joining the college, they worked hard and consistently ranked at the top of their class.

Calcutta, home to the Ganga, provided the visitors with an opportunity to bathe in its waters. They visited the Kalighat temple too.[151] During that time, Calcutta was populated by many wealthy and aristocratic people, such as Dwarakanath Tagore,[152] Raja Radhakanta Deb,[153] Raja Kalikrishna Deb, Prasanna Kumar Tagore,[154] Motilal Seal,[155] Akrur Dutta,[156] Ramkamal Sen,[157] Satyacharan Ghoshal, Rasamay Dutta, Madhab Chandra Bandopadhyay, Madhab Dutta and David Hare. The Phukans had the opportunity to meet with all of them, but Motilal Seal,

---

[150] The classes ran backwards. The last class before the school final was the first class those days.

[151] A famous temple of Goddess Kali in Calcutta.

[152] Dwarakanath tagore, the grandfather of Rabindranath Tagore, was a very wealthy industrialist.

[153] Radhakanta Deb, a scholar and a leader of the conservative Hindu society, co-founded Hindu College.

[154] Prasanna Kumar Tagore was a lawyer and a leader of the conservative Hindu society.

[155] Motilal Seal was a wealthy Bengali merchant and philanthropist.

[156] Akrur Dutta was a very influential and wealthy businessman.

[157] Ramkamal Sen was a banker, a lexicographer and the Secretary of the Asiatic Society, Calcutta.

in particular, took a liking to the boys, who had travelled from a faraway place to study. These boys were from an aristocratic family in Assam and had been recommended by the commissioner and his deputy. Moreover, their fathers had visited Calcutta, and a few people who knew them were still alive. Ananda Ram and Durgaram, the boys in question, conducted themselves with excellent manners and etiquette, which earned them the love and respect of everyone they encountered.

The group was captivated after touring notable landmarks like the mint, the Medical College and the fort.[158] The initial cohort of students from Assam who had travelled to Calcutta for their studies were excited by the arrival of Ananda Ram and Durgaram. A few of these students had chosen to study European medical practices but ultimately returned home after learning they would be required to perform dissections on corpses.

After the Phukans settled in Calcutta, Ramchandra Biswas returned to Bikrampur, and Matthie's attendant went back to Guwahati. The news of Ananda Ram and Durgaram's safe journey and admission to college brought much joy to their family back home and to the British officers. The Phukan brothers wrote weekly letters to their family, which took twelve days to reach Guwahati from Calcutta. However, our people were concerned about Calcutta as travellers often had difficulty adjusting to its

---

[158] Fort William, which was built in the early phase of the East India Company's administration in Calcutta.

climate. Sadly, Misir and Ananda Ram's servant died from fever and diarrhoea after a few months in Calcutta, adding to their family's worries.

A Brahmin named Radhakanta originally hailed from the village of Shila, near Barpeta in Kamrup district. After the British took control of the province, he migrated westwards. Radhakanta studied Sanskrit and various shastras,[159] including tantras, and was subsequently awarded the Nyayapanchanan[160] title. He was often referred to as Jotil or Jotiya Bhattacharjya due to his matted hair, or *jonta*. During this time, Radhakanta resided in Calcutta, where he became known for initiating a few Assamese boys who came to study there. He occasionally visited Phukan's residence, given his acquaintance with Ramdev[161] and his son. Radhakanta also re-initiated Durgaram at the Ganga strand.

Parashuram, the son of Mahodar Barua, and his friend Powal Chandra received support from Jenkins and Matthie to study in Calcutta. Ananda Ram was thrilled to reunite with Parashuram. Unfortunately, Durgaram fell ill with a fever in 1842, and despite intensive treatment, he passed away in August that year.[162] His last rites were performed on the banks of the Ganga. Durgaram was a

---

[159] Scriptures.

[160] An authority of Nyaya, a branch of Indian philosophy.

[161] Ramdev was Durgaram's Brahmin cook from Shila.

[162] In the original text, the date is the sixth day of the bright fortnight in the month of Saon, which may be converted as 12 August.

brilliant, handsome and healthy young man who had high expectations placed upon him by his country, but fate had other plans. As the saying goes, man proposes, and God disposes.

Ananda Ram was devastated by the loss of his companion. Durgaram's assistants and Ananda Ram's cook Shreedhar returned to Assam, leaving Ananda Ram feeling helpless and alone. He moved from Kolutola to Potoldanga, near the Hindu College, and employed a Bengali Brahmin cook. Until then, Ananda Ram had only eaten food prepared by an Assamese cook. Ramchandra Das Karmakar's son, Shyamcharan Das—a young man living in Calcutta's Potuatola Alley—became close friends with Ananda Ram and regularly visited him to provide care and education. His family also looked after Ananda Ram as one of their own, and others, such as Motilal Seal and Babu Nabin Chandra Karmakar, also provided support. Ananda Ram was in his adolescence, a time when boys often become restless and fearless, sometimes veering off course without proper guidance and care. Calcutta was a place full of both good and evil temptations. However, Ananda Ram was mindful of the temptations in Calcutta. He had Shyambabu as a friend, philosopher and guide, who helped him stay on the right path. Ananda Ram's classmates, including Sitanath Ghosh and Shibdas Dutta, were affectionate towards him. He could easily form a bond with Bengalis, as he spoke and understood the language well. His honesty was also appreciated by everyone.

The news of Durgaram's death hit Guwahati like a bombshell, plunging everyone into grief. Matthie and Jenkins were deeply saddened by the news as well. Ananda Ram's family had been troubled by premonitions before the Phukan brothers' departure, and sadly, their fears were realized with the deaths of Durgaram and his assistants. They grew increasingly worried about Ananda Ram. Even the British officers were unable to offer any further reassurances. Ananda Ram's mother, who had opposed the idea of sending her son to Calcutta from the start, was now even more anxious.

Ananda Ram's sister, Tuloshi, had recently reached puberty and undergone her second marriage ceremony.[163] Her husband took her to his home in Nagaon, causing Ananda Ram's mother and stepmother to worry even more. Each household employed a Bengali mukhtar to oversee their estates. Meanwhile, Balaram and Ranaram's sons, Gangaram and Gunabhiram, began attending school. However, a feud broke out between the two Phukan households over the ownership of four joint estates, including the Anandapur farm. Unfortunately, Ananda Ram lost the case. Both Phukan households stopped family maintenance payments to Ranaram, prompting him to file

---

[163] In the past, it was common for high-caste Hindus to practise child marriage. The first ceremony would take place before the bride reached puberty, and she would typically stay home. The second ceremony would occur after she had reached puberty, and she would then leave her home to live with her husband and in-laws.

a lawsuit for his share of the property, which was valued at Rs 79,000.[164] The case was refiled after initially being dismissed.

Balaram and Gangaram both underwent their sacred thread ceremony, with Balaram being initiated by his maternal grandfather, Kushadev Goswami, and Gangaram by his brother-in-law, Madhavram. Ananda Ram's mother requested Matthie and Jenkins to arrange for her son's return and wrote him a letter urging him to return.

At Hindu College, there were three departments: junior, senior and college. Students started in the junior department and then progressed to the senior department. To enter college, they had to pass the junior scholarship examination. Once in college, students had to pass the senior scholarship examination. At the beginning of 1844, Ananda Ram joined the third class of the senior department. His teacher, Ramchandra Mitra, took great care in teaching him. Other teachers, such as Ishwarchandra Saha, Gopikrishna Mitra, Joygopal Seth, Mr Eastjohn (sic),[165] Mr Jones[166] and Captain

---

[164] This incident happened before Ranaram's death.

[165] Most probably, he is T. Sturgeon, who taught in the senior department of Hindu College in 1843.

[166] R. Jones was the Headmaster of the Junior Department in Hindu College.

Richardson,[167] were pleased with Ananda Ram's excellent character and progress.

When he arrived in Calcutta, Ananda Ram had a hairstyle popular among boys—a shortcut with a tuft in the middle—which was fashionable while maintaining the Hindu custom. However, he later cut the tuft. Ananda Ram followed a daily routine of worshipping the Shaligram. He was fortunate to seldom experience significant illness, having only mild fever once, measles once and the occasional colds. He was careful about his diet and occasionally took a laxative. When Shreedhar Bapu and a servant named Ratia came to stay with him, they were joined by Haranath Choudhury from Kamrup and Shambhu, who had wandered into Calcutta. It was decided that Ananda Ram would return from Calcutta, and Parashuram's mother urged Matthie to allow her son's return, which was granted.

Ramchandra Biswas went to Calcutta, where his nephew, Kashichandra, studied, at Duff's school. Kashichandra, along with Powalchandra and Parashuram, decided to come to Assam with him. Before heading home, Ananda Ram bought several items, including books, tables, chairs, cupboards, couches, carpets, durries and palanquins. One day, while shopping at Burra Bazar,[168] Ramchandra loaded some items on a porter's head. As they walked

---

[167] Captain D.L. Richardson taught Literature and Ethics in Hindu College.

[168] Burra Bazar is a well-known wholesale market in Calcutta.

through the narrow alleys of Burra Bazar, crowded with pedestrians, carriages, palanquins and bullock carts, they got separated at a three-way junction. Ramchandra Biswas could not find the porter.

Lalbazar, a neighbourhood in Calcutta, was notorious for drunk British soldiers who resided in hotels and displayed uncivilized behaviour, causing nuisance to the pedestrians. One day, a drunken soldier jumped on to the carriage that Ramchandra and Ananda Ram were travelling in at Lalbazar. The soldier kicked Ramchandra when he protested before eventually leaving.

In late November 1844, Ananda Ram completed his shopping and met with nobles and acquaintances before booking a boat that could carry up to 600 maunds for his return journey. He loaded all his belongings onto the boat. Ananda Ram obtained certificates from his teachers and recorded the names of his classmates and friends. Had he stayed for two more years, he would have been eligible to take the junior scholarship examination. During his stay, he studied arithmetic, basic algebra concepts, the history of England, Rome, Greece and India, as well as an anthology of English poetry. Ananda Ram also learnt spoken English, English etiquette and the Bengali language with great precision.

As they sailed upstream through the Sundarbans, Ananda Ram and his group navigated through a forest that lies below sea level, south of Bakharganj in the Jashore district. In earlier times, this forest had been much more extensive. Sailing through the treacherous waters depended on the rise and fall of the tide. The journey was filled with danger, as crocodiles lurked in the water, tigers and buffaloes roamed the land, and robbers posed a threat. To ensure safety, Ananda Ram hired a Hindustani guard from Calcutta and brought along several large pots of fresh drinking water. Additionally, he made sure that everyone took turns staying awake at night. Despite the challenges, they successfully crossed the forest.

Ramchandra and Kashichandra urged Ananda Ram to visit their home. Ananda Ram stayed in Calcutta city and had never experienced the beauty of Bengal's countryside. Even when he was in Guwahati, he had only visited the villages of Beltola and Gog. Taking a detour to Bikrampur Pargana, Ananda Ram anchored the boat at Mirkashim's canal and stayed for three days in Ramchandra's native place, Betka. The locals mistook him for a king or landlord from Assam. Ananda Ram then continued his boat journey to Dhaka, visiting all the important places before resuming his voyage. Ramchandra's nephews, Kashichandra and Kalikrishna, also accompanied him, hoping to find jobs in Assam. Ramchandra went ahead on a smaller boat to attend to his duties and inform Ananda Ram's family of their arrival. The boat carried Parashuram Barua, Powalchandra, Kashichandra, Kalikrishna, Shreedhar, Haranath, Shambhu, Ratia, a guard and eight boatmen.

Meals, including lunch and dinner, were prepared on land. As it was winter, the daylight hours were shorter, making cooking and dining more time-consuming. Travelling by boat outside of a fleet at night was too risky due to the threat of robbers. Therefore, they hired a small flatboat[169] in Sirajganj to travel up to Goalpara. Sirajganj is a prominent commercial place in Bengal, situated on the Jamuna, a channel of the Brahmaputra. At any given time, approximately 3500 boats and ships from various countries were present in Sirajganj. Shreedhar, the cook, started preparing lunch on the flatboat early in the morning while the boat was still moving. By ten in the morning, the boat was anchored, and everyone had finished their meal before continuing the journey. Ananda Ram woke up early, got everyone ready, and ensured the day's travel began smoothly. He also helped with the sailing whenever the boat needed to stop. Since they had hired a new boat, they were able to travel faster than they had on their previous journey from Calcutta to Sirajganj.

During the voyage, Ananda Ram was constantly occupied with reading and writing. He often conversed with Parashuram and Kashichandra in English. One day, Parashuram, dressed in trousers and a *chapkan*,[170] strolled around the boat with his hands in his pockets, mimicking a European man's accent. However, he ended up falling off the boat's plank, which amused everyone. From that day on, Parashuram refrained from similar antics. The boat sailed upstream on the Brahmaputra, crossing Dhubri on its way to Rangamati. Rangamati was an ancient site where a high ranked official had been stationed when the region

---

[169] Palowar.

[170] A long, loose robe.

was under a Muslim nawab. It was situated on a hillside, and the Baruas of Rangamati, a landlord family that had known the Phukan clan since Brahmachari's days, lived there. The new Barua, Pratap Chandra, who had recently taken charge of the estate, sent many uncooked food items[171] and other provisions. Ananda Ram wished to meet the new Barua but needed bearers to carry his palanquin. The Baruas, however, did not have any. Kalikrishna fetched a few Mech[172] people from the hill where they lived, but Ananda Ram was concerned as his palanquin was hefty and required trained bearers.

Nonetheless, Pratap Chandra, his brother-in-law Gopinath, and his father Sadananda visited Ananda Ram. Sadananda, a record keeper at Hadirachoki during the days of Parashuram Barua and Brahmachari, shared many anecdotes from ancient times. The zamindar arrived in the afternoon with his entourage and a guard holding a baton. After paying their respects, they conversed for some time before Ananda Ram returned to his boat. They sailed upstream from Rangamati and reached Goalpara after three days. Several people, including Madhab Chandra Ghosh and Madhab Chandra Peshkar, came to meet Ananda Ram there. After taking a one-night break, they resumed sailing upwards. Ananda Ram posted letters back home and to

---

[171] The original word is *sidha*, which includes only uncooked provisions, as cooking and eating was a restricted and sacred ritual.

[172] An indigenous ethnic group from western Assam and across parts of Bengal.

his friends in Calcutta whenever and wherever he found a post office.

Ananda Ram's mother was overjoyed with the news of his homecoming. Tanuram Kakati from Nam Borbhag pargana was the mukhtar, and Gourakishore Poddar was the gomasta[173] of their gola. Both Kakati and Poddar cleaned the house and the yard with workers from their farms. They vacated the Chandi mandap, which had been used by Haliram Dhekial Phukan for worship and where a few bell-metal workers from Sarthebaris, including Kalamoni and Shreehari, resided at that time. These workers were sent to the nearby houses. It was decided that the Chandi mandap would serve as Ananda Ram's sitting room, so it was cleaned, and the interior sitting room was also tidied. Ramchandra had arrived early. Everyone was elated after receiving the news from him.

January had already arrived, and towards the end of the month[174] in 1845, the boat moored at around two in the afternoon. Many people from the nearby areas had gathered at the mooring site to witness the event. The neighbouring village's Kaivartas[175] had arrived with a band of drums and cymbals to add to the festive atmosphere. Ananda Ram was thrilled to see Gunabhiram and his merry group approaching the boat. Gunabhiram still did not have all his

---

[173] Accountant-cum-shopkeeper.

[174] The month of Magh.

[175] The so-called 'lower caste' people whose main livelihood was fishing.

teeth, and Ananda Ram was pleased with the progress in his studies. The band began to play with great enthusiasm, but Ananda Ram requested Kashiram to ask them to stop playing. However, the crowd refused, saying, 'Our Lord[176] can do as he pleases, but we will surely celebrate today.' The band had not been hired; they had come to the event on their own. Previously, they had served at every Phukan household celebration without any payment as they were attached to the family. Now, their farmhands carried Ananda Ram's palanquin home. A welcoming party of around 200–300 people had gathered. Ananda Ram got down from the palanquin and entered his home after bowing down to the idols of Gopal and Ganesh, accompanied by his guard. As the crowd tried to follow him inside, Ananda Ram asked them not to. His mother, with tears in her eyes, hugged and kissed him in the middle of the path.

Ananda Ram bowed down to greet his mother, grandmother, stepmother and other elders before visiting Balaram Phukan. Unfortunately, Balaram's mother had left for their estate a few days earlier. She had departed because she feared that seeing Ananda Ram would remind her of the loss of her son Durgaram, who had accompanied Ananda Ram to Calcutta but never returned. Ananda Ram met with Balaram and his other grandmother before returning home with Balaram. On the day of his return, Ananda Ram was dressed in a paisley-bordered dhoti from

---

[176] The original word is *Deuta*, which literally means father, also used in addressing a respectable man in Assam; sir; my Lord.

Santipur[177] paired with a short jacket, a shawl and shoes with socks. After enjoying light refreshments, he ventured out to the Chandi mandap.

As the boat arrived, people began unloading the belongings. A large crowd had gathered to welcome Ananda Ram, making it feel like a festive occasion. The people of Guwahati, particularly those in Bharalumukh, were ecstatic and overjoyed by Ananda Ram's return, despite being in mourning after Durgaram's death. Ananda Ram was occupied with conversing with his guests and overseeing the placement of his possessions. Some items were taken indoors, while others were arranged at the mandap. Matthie, at this time, was not in Guwahati and had travelled to Upper Assam.

The next day Ananda Ram went to meet Captain Jenkins, taking Balaram with him. While meeting Jenkins, he was dressed in *pantaloon*, chapkan and a cap. Unlike others, who left their shoes outside when meeting the captain, Ananda Ram did not do the same. Jenkins was delighted upon meeting him and made a huge fuss over him. Ananda Ram returned home after that.

Ananda Ram divided the Chandi mandap into three separate rooms. The front room was furnished with a floor bed, a mattress and large cushions, and was used for entertaining local gentlemen. In another room, he arranged chairs, tables and a couch. All the books that he had brought

---

[177] Santipur in West Bengal is known for handloom dhotis and sarees with intricate borders.

back from Calcutta were placed in four bookcases in that room, which was then used to receive his foreign guests. The third room, on the east side, served as his study. It was furnished with a table, chairs, a couch and a long wall bag of red, coarse cotton[178] to keep his letters organized. Although he initially used the interior sitting room as his bedroom, he later moved his bed to the main house. It took a few days to set up and organize the living quarters, and this type of furniture arrangement and interior decoration was the first of its kind among the natives of Guwahati. The reception arrangement was suitable for everyone. Ananda Ram also created a library-like system for his books, arranging them thematically. He systematically set up ink pots, pens, papers and penknives on his study table. He arranged for palanquin bearers from the estates but also bought a buggy.

Ananda Ram had been adored by everyone for his pleasant demeanour since childhood. Notably, as the son of Haliram Dhekial Phukan, he had returned after studying in Calcutta, which was considered as grand as London at the time. Numerous visitors, both locals and foreigners, came to meet him. When discussing Calcutta, he would often exclaim, 'Your eyes would pop out if you saw that!' Many people flocked to him thanks to his lineage, kind nature and the accomplishment of returning safely from Calcutta. Every morning and evening, large groups gathered to see him. However, our people typically do not value time and

---

[178] The original word was *kharua*, a red coarse cotton cloth sourced from outside Assam.

tend to stay without considering the host's needs, only leaving when they are bid farewell. For the first few days following Ananda Ram's arrival, he spent much of his time meeting with his audience and guests at home.

The festival of Holi was approaching, and recently, there had been a theft in which a crown belonging to Gopal—a revered deity in the house—and other items were stolen. Ananda Ram used the common fund to order a new gold crown for Gopal, modelled after the queen's crest from Tuti Sonari[179] in Sualkuchi. That year's Holi celebration was grander than previous years'. Ananda Ram's sister and her husband visited Guwahati upon hearing of his return, and Ananda Ram was overjoyed to see them. Later, Matthie also returned to Guwahati and was delighted to reunite with Ananda Ram after a long time.

At that time, a pastor named Robert Bland,[180] was present in Guwahati. He had graduated from Oxford [sic][181] and was highly knowledgeable. Matthie introduced

---

[179] Goldsmith.

[180] Reverend Robert James Bland studied in Jesus College, University of Cambridge, and worked as Chaplin of the Bengal Service. He was in India between 1843 and 1865. (John Venn & John Archibald Venn ed., *Cantabrigienses: A Biographical List of All Known Students, Graduates and Holders of Office at the University of Cambridge, from the Earliest Times to 1900*, Cambridge: Cambridge University Press, 2011, p. 294; *The Asiatic Journal and Monthly Register for British India and Its Dependencies*, vol. I, May–October, 1843, p. 315.)

[181] Robert James Bland graduated from Cambridge. See the previous note.

Ananda Ram to him, after which he began visiting the pastor daily to study. Bland's teachings expanded Ananda Ram's knowledge beyond what he had learned in Calcutta. Occasionally, in the morning or evening, Ananda Ram would also teach English to Balaram, Gangaram, Gunabhiram, and Prithuram Barua's son, Rudraram.

In the early morning, Ananda Ram would wake up and freshen up before getting dressed in his trousers, chapkan, hat, shoes and socks. Holding a walking stick, he would then go for a walk, often accompanied by Gunabhiram or others like Gangaram or Balaram. Ananda Ram preferred to take a secluded route rather than a crowded one. Upon returning, he would meet his visitors or study. He would usually shower around 9 a.m., followed by morning rituals and breakfast. He would then move to his sitting room, dressed in pyjamas and chapkan, and study in the reading room until the afternoon. He often had his afternoon snacks before going for a ride in his buggy car or strolling outside. Tea would be taken in the evening, followed by evening rituals around 8–9 p.m. and dinner. Ananda Ram would retire to bed around 9.30–10 p.m. He would visit both foreigners and native gentlemen. He would occasionally meet Parashuram Barua, his best friend. Every day, he memorized a section of Johnson's dictionary[182] and often studied with Pastor Bland at his home.

---

[182] *A Dictionary of the English Language* (1755) compiled by Samuel Johnson, also known as Johnson's Dictionary, is one of the most prominent early dictionaries of the English language.

Ananda Ram was known for his pleasant demeanour and respectful treatment of women, both within his family and outside of it. He gained the loyalty of many of his late father's staff, including Nanusingh Sikh of Phulara and Khargharia Phukan's bearer, Madhu. However, Tanuram Kakati was dismissed from his service due to actions that annoyed Ananda Ram. Ramchandra Biswas took over the management of the estates and farms under his direction. Ananda Ram's mother was the sole custodian of the keys to the lockers, among other items, but he helped relieve her burden after returning from Calcutta.

Worship and rituals continued as usual, and the construction of the house was nearly complete. Ananda Ram did not waste a single moment and studied daily. He was careful about eating sparsely, using only a small bowl to avoid overeating. He refrained from all intoxicants and refused to consume betel nuts, which he found unappealing, though he offered them and tobacco to his guests. He also visited Nilachal and Bashistha to offer his prayers. His character and behaviour pleased everyone, and no one labelled him a renegade. His Holi musical concert inspired others to follow his example. Many Assamese people began imitating his style.

Ananda Ram was so punctual that he kept a diary to record his daily routine briefly. He did not play any games and had forgotten those he played as a boy. He spoke to everyone with consideration for their age and profession and systematically kept his things in their assigned places. In summary, Ananda Ram's lifestyle became an inspiration for everyone around him.

Chapter 2

When Ananda Ram returned from Calcutta at the age of sixteen, he had grown a beard and moustache and started shaving, which gave him the appearance of a young man. At five feet three inches tall, he had a healthy build. As he was the only son, his family members had been planning his marriage even before he returned from Calcutta. They searched for a suitable bride in Guwahati and other places but were unsuccessful. Although Ananda Ram did not prefer child marriage, he believed that getting married at his age would be better than living a wayward life. He was aware that marriage could safeguard his well-being, provided he took care of himself. He aspired to maintain this equilibrium. His personality reassured his British acquaintances that he would not mishandle his marriage. They urged him to get married, and he heeded their advice.

During ancient times, the Indravanshi[183] or Ahoms, a non-Aryan tribe, did not practise the Vedic religion.

---

[183] They believed that they descended from heaven. That is why they called themselves a clan related to Indra, a heavenly god and their king was addressed as Swargadeo or a God from heaven.

However, they were introduced to the Vedic way of life during the reign of King Siva Singha, and since then, they abandoned their non-Vedic rituals. Consequently, they required gurus and priests. The king became a disciple of Parbatiya Gosain[184] and appointed a Brahmin family of Gautama gotra from upper Assam as priests. This family became royal priests or Rajgurus, commonly known as Rajguru Phukan. After the British annexation, a Rajguru Phukan named Pashupati came to Guwahati and was appointed as Lakheraj Panchayat[185] in the revenue branch at the commissionerate. Later, his wife, Kamaleswari Phukanani, arrived in Guwahati with their two daughters, Chandri and Mahindri. They had a son named Durgachandra and another daughter named Brajasundari while residing in Panbazar, neighbours to Madhavram Bora and Gobindaram Nazir. Panbazar was a busy area, with numerous shops and foreign officials' residences.

Pashupati was a sincere, reliable and gentle person who dutifully performed daily rituals. He would often invite and feed guests on any occasion. His wife embodied the ideal qualities expected of a wife, such as welcoming guests, preparing and serving food, and taking care of household items. Chandri was wedded to Homeshwar, the youngest son of Munshef Lakkhidatta Borkotoki, while Mahindri remained at home to assist her parents with household chores, which she had been doing from a young age. She

---

[184] See Chapter 1.

[185] A jury member of the committee in charge of revenue-free land.

also learnt how to make yarn from cotton and weave. In those days, there was little emphasis on teaching girls how to read, write or do embroidery. Mahindri's mother taught her how to worship, perform other rituals, manage kitchen work and make sweets.

Pashupati's family often welcomed both local and foreign guests for various celebrations. Mahindri dutifully attended to these guests as instructed by her parents. She was intelligent and quick to learn, earning the admiration of those around her for her honesty and good behaviour. However, as she grew older, her parents began to worry about finding her a suitable husband. Despite receiving numerous proposals, including one to marry Ananda Ram while he was in Calcutta, they had yet to accept any. Another proposal came from Parashuram, but Pashupati remained undecided. He desired an equal match for his beautiful and talented daughter and thus continued his search.

A group of people believed that the Phukan family had lost their status because they behaved like the British. People thought less of those who had close relationships with Muslims and the British. The Phukan family regarded the British as equals. Additionally, they had incorporated a few foreign customs and products into their lives, which were harmless. Although they had connections with local elites, some people still criticized them, but not in public. This was an open secret in the conservative society of Assam. However, the Phukans had not lost the earlier glory of their family and caste.

A proposal was made for Ananda Ram to marry Mahindri, and Pashupati was pleased with the idea but had yet to decide. Some people warned him against accepting the proposal, but sensible men like Jenkins and Matthie encouraged him to accept Ananda Ram as his son-in-law. Ananda Ram had met Mahindri as a child when he visited Parashuram, and Parashuram had spoken highly of her beauty and skills. After learning more about her, Ananda Ram was not opposed to the alliance. Pashupati had known Ananda Ram from the time of his birth and was aware of his excellent character and achievements in Guwahati and Calcutta. After Ananda Ram returned from Calcutta, Pashupati learnt of his honesty. Pashupati's wife, a friend of Balaram's mother, was well aware of Ananda Ram and happily agreed to the proposal. According to their horoscopes, Ananda Ram and Mahindri were moderately compatible. One day, Pashupati visited Ananda Ram's home and conversed with Ananda Ram and his grandmother. He then announced the engagement, stating, 'I am not taking anyone's opinion into consideration. I am offering Mahindri Aiti's[186] hand to Anandi Bapa.'[187] The families and friends of the bride and groom were filled with joy.

The wedding, scheduled for April–May[188] 1844,[189] was a well-planned celebration that lasted five days. In

---

[186] A term of affection used in addressing or speaking of a girl.

[187] A term affectionately addressed to a boy or a young man.

[188] Bohag.

[189] 1767 Sak.

anticipation of the wedding, several musical soirées were held, including one for foreign guests. Unfortunately, on the day of the foreign guests' soirée, a fireworks display resulted in a near-disastrous fire that almost burnt down the house. Despite this and some minor inconvenience caused by rain on the wedding night, the ceremony proceeded without a hitch. Ananda Ram, dressed in a pajama with *zari* work and an *anga* topi, travelled to his in-laws' place on an exquisitely decorated Tamjang palanquin[190] and changed into silk clothes[191] before the rituals began.

Traditionally, the bridegroom covers his nose with a handkerchief[192] and avoids speaking with the father-in-law. Even after the wedding, the groom typically has limited interaction with his wife's relatives.

It is usually difficult to hear the groom's chants during the wedding ceremony, but Ananda Ram was not timid. He respectfully and openly spoke with his father-in-law during the hom ritual. Some people labelled him as shameless for this, but it only revealed their narrow-mindedness. After the *dwiragaman*[193] celebration, the bride returned to her

---

[190] Tamjang or Tonjon is an open sedan chair used in India and Sri Lanka and carried by a single pole on men's shoulders.

[191] Patta-vastra.

[192] This act is considered a sign of bashfulness.

[193] The ceremony of a newlywed bride coming from her paternal abode for the second time to her husband's house. Usually, a bride permanently stays at her husband's home. However, a child bride returns to her parental home and waits till she attends puberty.

father's home. She attained puberty next Jeth,[194] but the second marriage ceremony had to be postponed as puberty occurred at an inauspicious moment.[195] It was later performed in Kati,[196] and Ananda Ram finally brought his wife home.

The delay caused by the inauspicious timing turned out to be a blessing for Ananda Ram. He had not prepared a suitable living space for himself and his future wife before their marriage. He used the extra time they had to create a comfortable home for their life together.

Typically, the arrival of a new daughter-in-law is a cause for celebration, but it can also lead to non-stop gossip and scrutiny of every single move she makes. This can create tension in the household and spoil domestic bliss. However, Mahindri was fortunate enough to avoid such negativity. Her mothers-in-law, aunts-in-law and grandmothers-in-law all adored her and affectionately trained her without finding fault. This positive attitude was contagious, and other household members followed suit. Ananda Ram also cherished her, and she quickly became the apple of everyone's eye.

Ananda Ram was aware of the societal norm that forbade girls from studying at their parental home. However,

---

[194] May–June.

[195] In Hindu astrology, some days and moments are believed to be inauspicious and to nullify the ill omens, one has to observe certain rituals.

[196] October–November.

he recognized the importance of education and decided to become a teacher to his wife himself. He commenced teaching her, and with the support of other literate women in the family, she was encouraged to learn. Mahindri was appointed as the assistant to Ananda Ram's stepmother, who was in charge of the kitchen.

In Aghon,[197] Tuloshi gave birth to a baby boy named Chandrahas after a long and difficult labour. Following Ananda Ram's wedding, it was Balaram's turn to tie the knot. He was marrying Gopali, Munshef Madhuram Khound's daughter from Nagaon. Ananda Ram took charge of planning and coordinating the wedding, which included procuring exotic items from the West, including Rangpur and creating exquisite outfits. Performers from Rangpur and Goalpara, including courtesans, kettle drummers, bands and drummers,[198] as well as local groups like drummers, *gayan-bayan*,[199] *ojapali*[200] and *hajowalia*,[201] were hired to entertain the guests. Everyone was invited. The wedding celebrations lasted sixteen days, culminating in a grand fireworks display. From Bharalumukh to Fancy Bazar, the entire area was illuminated with rows of lamps, and both local and foreign guests were treated to sumptuous feasts. The court even remained closed for two days.

---

[197] November–December.

[198] Both *dhak* and *dhol* are types of drums.

[199] A band of traditional musicians.

[200] A traditional choir or party of singers.

[201] Musical performers based from Hajo school of music.

The wedding was held on 3 February,[202] a Wednesday. That day, the groom went for a ride on a palanquin.[203] Upon arriving home, a sudden heavy rainstorm dampened the fun and celebration. Nevertheless, the wedding rituals were completed, and everyone agreed they had never seen such an extravagant wedding. Sadly, Balaram's new wife passed away shortly after the wedding.

Ananda Ram, a devoted family man, was searching for a way to maintain a respectable lifestyle after losing several family properties. He decided to become a judge and began studying law. At the time, Chandrasen Bharali Kakati was the principal sadar amin in Guwahati, with Somadatta Kataki and Madhavram Rajkhowa as munshefs. Devabar Bordoloi was the sadar amin, and Lakkhidatta Kataki was a direct munshef. These judges would happily conduct trials while sitting on a wooden platform, reclining on cushions and occasionally enjoying betel nuts. The clerks recorded statements from witnesses and presented other documents to the judges. Advocates had little prestige back then. Still, lawyers such as Shibcharan Deb, Biswanath Guha, Kamalakanta Sarkhel, Bagaram Borah, Dhiranath Sarmah, Haramohan Pandit, Ramananda Bhattacharjya and others argued their cases while sitting on the same platform. They asked questions during the recording of witness statements, and even clerks were allowed to make a point or two for

---

[202] The original text mentioned the first day of Aghon, which may be converted to 3 February.

[203] *Choudol* is a palanquin that has four bearers.

the plaintiff or defendant before the judge. Distinguished visitors witnessing the trial could also share their views with a judge or clerk. After disclosing a few observations, the judges either decreed, dismissed or non-suited a case or punished the defendant. The head clerk or bench clerk noted the entire proceeding, from filing the lawsuit to the judgment, with a summary of the argument. Sometimes, a court case took a long time to be resolved. This was the judicial system at that time.

Matthie sahab and Jenkins sahab advised Ananda Ram to learn about the law and court proceedings from the principal sadar amin. Ananda Ram took their advice and regularly visited the court to observe judicial proceedings and documents while studying the law and Assam's judicial rules at home. With each passing day, Ananda Ram's knowledge and skills improved.

During that time, only a few people in Guwahati knew English, and Ananda Ram helped by making English translations of applications and drafting replies to notices and other papers. One critical court case involved the trustees of the Hayagriv Madhav temple and Lakshmiballabh Goswami over the temple administration. Ananda Ram revised and translated the trustees' papers for the case without the expectation of any reward or fee. He always intended to support the victim and offer his assistance.

After Haliram's death, Jagyaram Khargharia Phukan managed the affairs of both households when Ananda Ram was still too young. Ananda Ram had a minor grievance, which he conveyed to their mutual friend, Matthie. To resolve the issue, Matthie appointed mediators, including Chandrasen, the principal sadar amin, and Shambhunath Bagchi, the sheristadar, at the collectorate. They successfully negotiated a solution.

Ananda Ram began writing for *Orunodoi*, a monthly journal first published in 1846 from Sivasagar. He believed that a country could only progress if it used its local language. Assamese had once been the language used for all purposes in the region. However, after the government declared Bengali as the actual language of the region, it began to be used for all purposes. Observing the difficulties this created for both the judiciary and the public, Ananda Ram strove to revive the use of the Assamese language. He wrote a two-volume book called *Asamiya Lorar Mitra*,[204] based on several English educational texts. He sent the manuscript to the Samachar Chandrika Press in Calcutta, but the printers struggled to decipher Assamese. As a result, Ananda Ram sent Kirtikanta Barua, an Assamese speaker, to Calcutta. The book was eventually published in 1849, thanks to donations from both British and native patrons. Matthie and Jenkins had greatly encouraged Ananda Ram in this endeavour.

There is no need to reiterate how passionate Ananda Ram was about developing the Assamese language, but his efforts saw little progress during his lifetime. However, after overcoming many hurdles, Assamese finally became

---

[204] *The Friend of Young Assam.*

the language of the land in 1872 (sic),[205] by order of Lieutenant Governor George Campbell. An abridged version of Ananda Ram's *Asamiya Lorar Mitra* has become a textbook in schools of this province.

The progress of the Assamese language owes much to Ananda Ram. He reasoned with everyone who supported or opposed the language issue and remained in constant touch with missionaries, whether in person or by correspondence, during their efforts to promote the language. Ananda Ram will always be remembered for his contributions, irrespective of the rise or decline of the Assamese language.

Prithuram, Gobindaram and Gangaram, sons of Shambhuram Barua, initiated legal action against the Phukan family to obtain their share of the property. However, their case was dismissed. No other significant legal disputes arose after this. Following the death of his first wife, Balaram married Bishnupriya, the daughter of Rajmedhi from Nadala in Kamrup.

During a visit to one of his farms at Bangalgaon, Pashupati fell ill and passed away. Shortly afterwards, his wife also passed away. They left behind a son, Durgachandra, aged nine, and a daughter, Brajasundari, aged four. Ananda Ram and Mahindri brought the two orphans and all their belongings home. Joymoti, a Brahmin widow, and Kaniki, a maid, joined them. As the Phukans had no children of their own, the kids helped fill the void to some extent. The

---

[205] It could be a printing mistake. The Assamese language was reinstated as a court language and medium of instruction in 1873.

children were cared for with love and attention, which helped them cope with the loss of their parents and eased the grief.

Ranaram had two sons by two wives. Gangaram, the elder, was born to the first wife, while Gunabhiram, the younger, was born to the second. Gangaram left his studies and took over the management of Bangaon Mouza,[206] or Duwar, which was registered in his name. Later, he became a paymaster for the treasurer[207] at the criminal court. At the time, Gunabhiram was studying English at school. Gangaram initiated Gunabhiram into the scared thread ceremony during Balaram's first marriage. Ranaram's two wives did not get along well. The second wife and Gunabhiram began living independently in the same house, but struggled to make ends meet. Naduki, a dwarf maid who had accompanied Gunabhiram's mother from her parental home, and her daughter, Koniki, worked as labourers, contributing their wages to meet the household's daily expenses. Ananda Ram had a fondness for Gunabhiram and his mother, often inviting them for lunch and dinner while also covering their clothing expenses. In 1845,[208] Gunabhiram and Ananda Ram's sister, Tuloshi, accompanied Gunabhiram's mother on a visit to Nagaon

---

[206] A revenue division of a district under a collector of revenue called Mauzadar.

[207] Nazir is a native court official, who serves processes, acts as treasurer, and performs other similar duties.

[208] 1768 Sak.

to see her daughter. After a short stay, she returned to Guwahati, where she passed away on Ashokastami[209] in Chot[210] the following year. Gunabhiram then moved in with Gangaram, who had married Bidya, daughter of Somdatta Kataki, in 1846.[211] Even though Gunabhiram lived with Gangaram, Ananda Ram continued to take care of him in every possible way. Gunabhiram received a monthly allowance of three rupees from Jenkins and remained a constant and deferring companion to Ananda Ram.

Ananda Ram had a profound interest in learning about ancient history and its associated stories since childhood. He would eagerly listen to any elderly person willing to share their knowledge. One such figure was Atiram Barua from Sundaridiya, who had become influential after the British took over Assam. However, he later fell ill and lived in misery in Guwahati. Despite his condition, Atiram remained courageous and never hesitated to speak his mind. He would often visit Ananda Ram. Jogai Thakur, the *tamuly*[212] of Parashuram Barua, had come from Naduwar with his son to see Ananda Ram. Ananda Ram was always captivated by tales of the old days, which he also learnt from his female relatives. However, he would sometimes become lost in his thoughts and ended up having the stories repeated. At times, he became so absorbed in his thoughts

---

[209] The eighth day of the bright fortnight in the month of Chot.

[210] March–April.

[211] 1769 Sak.

[212] Tamuly is an attendant of a noble who serves betel nut.

that if someone asked him a question, he would either not respond or simply mutter a 'hmm' in acknowledgement. He would then have the person repeat whatever they were saying. On one such occasion, Atiram was recounting a story, which ended without Ananda Ram realizing. After a pause, Ananda Ram asked what happened next, only to be told the story had already concluded. Amused, he burst into laughter. He was always contemplating the future, a habit that often left him absent-minded.

Ananda Ram performed the shraddha ritual to honour his father, grandfather and great-grandfather. He offered daily tarpan[213] and food to his ancestors in the preceding fortnight, followed by a Parvan Shraddha[214] at Mahalaya.[215] Additionally, he conducted the Navanna Shraddha[216] ritual. All other annual ceremonies continued as usual. Both households performed daily worship of their household deity, Gopal, every other month.

Ananda Ram was highly respected by all judges, and many believed he could make anything happen simply by making a request. Many individuals sought his help, but he refused, as he disliked persuasion. Despite his firm stance, some selfish individuals continued to bother him, but he remained

---

[213] A Hindu ritual to offer drinking water to the ancestors or deities.

[214] A Hindu ceremony performed in honour of deceased ancestors during special occasions.

[215] The new moon day before Durga Puja.

[216] Navanna Shraddha is performed during the harvest season to offer new grains to the ancestors.

resolute in his unwillingness to entertain such requests. He clearly stated that he could not intervene and often explained that, in many cases, a simple application was sufficient.

Ananda Ram's residence would often be frequented by schoolchildren, whom he encouraged to study diligently. At the time, English was still perceived as an alien language. Consequently, the number of students in the Bengali school was much higher than in the English school. The common understanding was that education merely meant learning enough Bengali to write an application and carrying a pen behind one's ear to the courts. Young boys from well-known families were often sent to apprentice in the courts, where they outnumbered the clerks. They would earn a few rupees daily, which they would take home. However, Ananda Ram strongly disapproved of this apprentice class and considered their profession as inferior.

In order to complete their education, one needed to learn Persian. Those who could recite a few lines of Persian poetry in conversations were often praised, as the beauty and charm of Persian poetry would make someone stand out and be seen as captivating. Ananda Ram received instruction in Urdu and Persian from a *munshi* for a while, studying up to *Gulistan*[217] and *Bostan*.[218] He had almost

---

[217] A classical medieval Persian prose text composed by the Persian poet Shaikh Saadi Shirazi in 1258 CE.

[218] Another classical medieval Persian text by Shaikh Saadi Shirazi in 1257 CE.

all of the *Pand Nama*[219] memorized. Ananda Ram was introduced to Tantra by the renowned *tantric* Gopinath Choudhury, who lived in East Bajali pargana.

During the winter season, a performer of *gosai kirtan*[220] named Chandrakumar Goswami from Uthali would visit Guwahati and earn a significant income by performing *kirtans* at different households almost every Sunday. Sometimes, *jatra*[221] performers from the West would also make money performing at a few places. Ananda Ram would also organize kirtans and jatras at his house; and the attendees of this event offered tips to the performers. He too accepted almost all such invitations. Although Ananda Ram was not particularly interested in music and did not support spending money on such things, he nevertheless believed it should be encouraged as a part of social life.

At that time, people generally did not depend on doctors for medical treatment. However, a Hindustani physician named Shital Singh lived in Guwahati and served in the army. Ananda Ram, who had once recovered under Singh's care, appointed him as the family doctor. Though Ananda Ram had no major illnesses, he would consult Singh for minor ailments and take the prescribed medicines. He also did the same for other family members. On one occasion, Singh successfully treated a boil on Ananda Ram through

---

[219] A classical medieval Persian text authored by Hazrat Sheikh Farid-al-Din Attar.

[220] Act of singing in praise of god.

[221] A folk song and drama form.

medication and surgery. Balaram and Parashuram also
began seeking treatment from Singh, and before long,
many others came to depend on him for medical advice
and prescriptions.

Ananda Ram had been a student of Reverend Bland,
who conducted Sunday services at the church. Although
Ananda Ram attended a few such services, he was not
regarded as a renegade. He did not believe that going to a
prayer service was a sin.

When Ananda Ram started attending court regularly
to learn the trade, he changed his attire. He swapped his
hat for an official turban and added a shawl over his anga
or chapkan with a pajama. This change was necessitated
by his having to sit on a platform and leave his shoes on
the floor, and wearing trousers was uncomfortable in this
seating arrangement. Therefore, he changed his style to one
that was more suitable.

Part II

Chapter 3

Until then, Ananda Ram had been relying on his ancestral property for his livelihood. The absence of an income made spending feel like a punishment, and he found it increasingly difficult to maintain a lifestyle befitting his illustrious family. Despite living frugally, his expenses increased day by day. He discouraged extravagance and kept his own accounts. Although food grains and other items came from the estates and farms, they proved insufficient. His father had not left much behind due to his charitable contributions, and eventually their gola had to be shut down. Owing to all these reasons, Ananda Ram began to feel the pinch.

In those days, the *mouzadars*[222] and choudhurys from different parganas gained their wealth by levying taxes on their tenants. Some oppressed their tenants by usurping their land and granting it to others or by replacing existing officers arbitrarily. Others meted out punishment without valid cause. Occasionally, this oppression led people from

---

[222] The revenue collector of a mouza.

different parganas to travel to Guwahati with their leaders to file complaints against the choudhurys. Additionally, some choudhurys misled the government by failing to report newly cultivated land. These issues became a serious concern for the authorities, who resolved to appoint a young, trustworthy custodian to address the situation.

Matthie and Jenkins suggested that Ananda Ram join the service as a custodian of a pargana. This experience would greatly benefit his future career, as he would learn more about the tenants, circumstances, the agricultural practices of the farmers and produce, as well as land settlement and surveys. After giving it some thought, Ananda Ram accepted the post.

Early in 1847, Digambar Barua, the munshef of Rangia, passed away. At the time, character, lineage and general efficiency were the only criteria for employment. The commissioner would write down the names of three aspirants. The first was appointed to the vacant position. The list always contained three names. Following this rule, Radhakanta Barua, the custodian of the Khata Pargana, was appointed munshef in place of Digambar Barua. Ananda Ram was appointed custodian of Khata Pargana by Order Number 1123, issued by Collector Agnew[223] of Kamrup District on 29 April 1847. He was directed to deposit the estimated revenue, collected from landholders by the serving officers of pargana, to the government. He was also directed not to oppress the farmers and to obey all orders

---

[223] W. Agnew.

from the authorities. His appointment was well received and appreciated by all.

Most of the choudhurys in the parganas were descendants of Kamrup's renowned choudhury clan. They were highly respected, admired by people. When travelling to the office, they used a borjapi and were accompanied by a group of bearers who carried their hookah, fire, *lota*[224] and *thonga*.[225] While returning home from the pargana, they used a palanquin and were accompanied by many people. These people who served the choudhurys did not receive a salary but hoped to be granted a small exemption in the revenue for their land. However, when Ananda Ram became custodian, he relieved the people of Khata Pargana of these obligations. He did not fire any officer without reason, and revenue collections became prompt. He directly inquired after the problems of his tenants and resolved them. He also introduced a system of organizing and keeping documents.

Previously, people would bring gifts when visiting the choudhury, and they also offered presents during festivals and special occasions. Many even bribed him into being enlisted in the upper class to get relief from obligatory service without a wage.[226] However, Ananda Ram did not encourage such practices, and everyone remained satisfied under his charge. Those who tried to find fault with Ananda

---

[224] A metal water pot.

[225] A coarse woollen blanket used for seating.

[226] In the original text, *Begar* (forced labour system) is used.

Ram were not successful. While working as a custodian, he did not neglect his law studies or other responsibilities. He even found time to compose his book *Asamiya Lorar Mitra*.

Ananda Ram, with his enlightened mind, struggled to adapt to the rustic and unrefined custodianship of a pargana custodian. During this time, he heard that the post of translator at Jenkins' agency office would be available soon. The current translator, Becher,[227] planned to resign and start his own business. Ananda Ram wanted the job and requested Jenkins to consider him for the position. Jenkins promised that he would be considered if the opportunity arose. However, the position did not become available. Ananda Ram had been eager to take the job as it would allow him to learn about local and foreign affairs, which aligned with his interest in diverse topics. He believed that knowledge was key to becoming charismatic.

Matthie was a devoted friend to the region and always had the development of the local people on his mind. In the previous year, a government steamer had sailed to Guwahati. On one occasion, Matthie sahab invited several Assamese people aboard the vessel for a cruise, showcasing its various machines. Ananda Ram was among the guests.

That winter, Matthie decided to travel to Calcutta. Jagannath Bordoloi, the munshef at Nalbari, along with his clerks Brajanath Phukan and Gobindaram Sharma, expressed their interest in accompanying him. Matthie agreed to take them at his own expense. Jagannath munshef

---

[227] W. Becher later became a planter.

applied for three months' leave, and Matthie wrote to Ananda Ram recommending him as acting munshef for the duration of the leave. Ananda Ram was at the top of the list of aspirants for the position. Matthie advised him to ignore the meagre salary, as serving that post, even for a few days, would benefit him while applying for a permanent high position. He asked Ananda Ram to respond promptly so that he could issue the necessary order. At the time, Ananda Ram was in the pargana collecting tax when he received Matthie's letter. He accepted the offer gladly and without hesitation, and then returned to Guwahati. On 16 November, Dalton,[228] the chief assistant commissioner, issued an order appointing Ananda Ram as acting munshef for three months. After joining the service, Ananda Ram went to Nalbari and took charge. At the time, a munshef's salary was Rs 80, with an additional Rs 40 allocated for hiring a head clerk,[229] a record keeper,[230] a proceeding writer,[231] a judgment writer[232] and a translator.[233] This amount could also be used for contingency expenses. However, Ananda Ram's monthly salary as an acting munshef was only Rs 40.

Ananda Ram took charge as a judge and began presiding over legal disputes. He did not rely on his clerks

---

[228] E.T. Dalton.

[229] *Chirastadar.*

[230] *Peshkar.*

[231] *Roobkar-nabis.*

[232] *Faisala-nabis.*

[233] *Nakal-nabis.*

to write the judgments but reviewed the documents himself. His first ruling was a dismissal. At that time, the courts paid little attention to grammar, making it challenging to comprehend the rulings. Ananda Ram changed this system by writing his judgments in simple language, making them easy to understand. His orders were well received by people. After completing his tenure, Ananda Ram handed over his responsibilities to Munshef Bordoloi and returned to Guwahati. The clarity and reasoning of his decrees fascinated lawyers, clerks and judges alike, and resulted in successful outcomes for cases that went for appeals.

Upon his return to Guwahati, Ananda Ram resumed his studies and training. At that time, the commissioner of Assam had three types of assistants: chief assistant, sub-assistant and junior assistant. Junior assistants were gazetted officers recruited from the army, with the possibility of promotion to chief assistant commissioner. Sub-assistant commissioners, however, were not gazetted, and no native had yet been appointed to that rank. To apply, candidates had to go through a test held by a committee set up by the commissioner. If selected, the government appointed the candidates with the commissioner's approval. Ananda Ram studied law rigorously to appear in this examination. He even considered taking the test in Bengal, intending to join the service there if he did not succeed in Assam.

In September 1848, Kirtinath Khangia Phukan, the munshef at Barpeta, went on six months' leave following Dussehra. Jagannath Bordoloi, munshef of Nalbari, was transferred to Barpeta. Ananda Ram was reappointed as the acting munshef at Nalbari. He resumed his duties there during the winter of that year and became more proficient in judicial services this time. He returned to Guwahati after completing the term.

Afterwards, Ananda Ram submitted an application to Jenkins, the commissioner and agent to the governor, seeking to sit for the examination for selection as a sub-assistant. The commissioner formed a committee comprising Deputy Commissioner Matthie and Chief Assistant Commissioner Dalton. The committee administered a series of tests to assess Ananda Ram's abilities, which included translating a Bengali application into English, translating a commissioner's letter into Bengali, reading and summarizing a document from the magistrate's office, answering questions related to civil, criminal and revenue laws of Bengal as well as temporary laws enforced in Assam.[234] Additionally, he was tested on surveying with a chain and compass, measuring land using a bamboo measuring pole and drawing maps.

Ananda Ram performed exceptionally well in all the tests. The committee also reviewed the documents related to the cases Ananda Ram had worked on as the acting munshef at Nalbari. They found his work satisfactory and submitted a report to the commissioner detailing the examinations conducted and their results. The report included Ananda Ram's translations, answer scripts and the map he had drawn. It also mentioned his lineage, the

---

[234] Assam *Kaydabandi*.

service record of his father and uncle, his character and his academic progress. The committee elaborated on his service record as the pargana custodian and as acting munshef, and recommended him as the most suitable candidate for the post. The commissioner was thrilled when he received this report.

The Vedic tradition prescribes various rituals for expectant women, which Ananda Ram's wife followed when she became pregnant. On 13 August 1849, she gave birth to a daughter named Rasheswari. Although society generally celebrated the birth of a son, some believed that a daughter as the firstborn was a good omen. Ananda Ram was not disappointed that his firstborn was a girl. He was grateful for whatever God had kindly granted him. At the time, Ananda Ram was nineteen years, eleven months and two days old, and Mahindri was sixteen.

When news of Pashupati and his wife's death reached their home in Jorhat, Balaram Deka Phukan brought Brajasundari and Durgachandra back to their hometown. Ananda Ram was left with the responsibility of their belongings and rent-free estates. Mahindri wished for Gunabhiram to marry Brajasundari, but it was not possible at the time, as the girl was too young, and the boy was still studying.

After the British government established control over the region, a deputy collector carried out a survey of all parganas and mouzas. Later, a survey officer conducted a scientific re-survey to finalize their boundaries. During this period, a sub-assistant named Bedford[235] undertook the survey in Goalpara district, with the help of his colleague Driver. Meanwhile, Vetch[236] and Brodie[237] from Lakhimpur and Sivasagar had to move towards the frontier to manage the Khamtis and the Nagas. As a magistrate was required during the survey period, Jenkins wrote a letter (no. 155, dated 16 July 1849) to the government recommending Ananda Ram's name. The commissioner also wrote satisfactorily about Ananda Ram's lineage, education and character. However, the letter did not yield any quick results.

Four hundred years ago, Biswasingha—renowned as a son of Shiva—had ascended the throne of Koch Bihar. One of his sons, Naranarayan, became king of Koch Bihar and Kamrup and built the Kamakhya temple on the Nilachal Hill. One of their descendants ruled Bijni, located north of Goalpara. The Bijni raja or chieftain was nearly autonomous in his kingdom, Nij Bijni, which included two parganas, Hawraghat and Khutaghat, under Muslim nawabs. When the British government acquired Bengal, Bihar and Odissa from the nawab of Bengal in 1765, the Bijni raja became a zamindar under British rule on account of these two parganas.

Amritnarayan Bhup was the Bijni raja when the present tale unfolded. Like other zamindars and chieftains, the Bijni

---

[235] James Bedford.

[236] Hamilton Vetch.

[237] T. Brodie.

raja also ruled with the help of a *dewan*[238] and other officers. Gradually, the relationship between the raja and his tenants deteriorated. He had taken out a huge loan, which grew yearly on account of the interest. Land settlements with his tenants had not been done adequately. Many occupied extensive stretches of land while paying only nominal rent, and others held much more land than had been given as donations, and so on. Many had large, long-overdue rents. Whenever the raja tried to file a case or reach a settlement, the tenants resorted to complaints. Both parties were now at loggerheads, and the raja became helpless. A few people sided with the tenants and continually opposed the raja's proposals, while he, in turn, refused to listen to their suggestions. The constant bickering had become a source of frustration for the government officers.

Ananda Ram's competence was widely recognized, so the raja's men nominated him as the dewan. The raja agreed, and his tenants raised no objections to this proposal. Even Jenkins, the commissioner of Assam and collector of Goalpara, supported Ananda Ram's appointment. The Bijni raja, a prominent figure in the country, had a long-standing relationship with the Duworiya family and owed money to them. As the dewan's position was elite and prestigious, Ananda Ram would gain both renown and influence by successfully diffusing the tension between the

---

[238] A financial manager or high official in the office of the estate of a zamindar.

raja and his tenants. Considering all these factors, Ananda Ram accepted the offer at a monthly salary of Rs 250.

The raja was delighted by the news, and Ananda Ram travelled to Bijni towards the end of 1849. He received the entitlements of his position, such as the sceptre and orderlies, and stayed in Parashuram's house in Goalpara after renovating the old house and constructing a new one. Ananda Ram then met with the raja, who entrusted him with full responsibility.[239]

Officials of the raja and others in the parganas did not follow any systematic method for documentation and record-keeping. The accounts of realized and unrealized revenue, rent rolls, statements of expenditure, and credit were recorded in an incomplete and haphazard manner. Calculations for the due payment of debts were not done correctly. Nor was there any distinct system for treasury dispatch. Everyone followed their own rules. Nij Bijni's administration was similarly chaotic. After consulting with all the officials of the parganas and reviewing the accounts, Ananda Ram became familiar with the situation.

Ananda Ram drafted a comprehensive set of rules and regulations to govern Nij Bijni. This list, known as *Phookan Dewanar Kaydabandi*,[240] detailed the procedures for revenue collection, maintenance of law and order, duties of judicial officers, and their rights of punishment.

---

[239] Of finding a solution regarding the ongoing stalemate or dispute between the zamindar and his subjects or tenants.

[240] *The Kaydabandi of Phookan Dewan.*

Additionally, he regulated the process of surveying and the settlement of farmlands, jungles, wastelands and winter rice land,[241] and made arrangements for the remittance of unpaid taxes. He also fixed the rates for water tax,[242] forest tax,[243] tolls for staking timbers on zamindar's land,[244] duties on jungle produce[245] and grazing tax[246] and arranged for the collection of those taxes from estates. Lastly, Ananda Ram assigned duties to the pargana's officials, including the rent collectors,[247] record keepers,[248] investigatory clerks,[249]

---

[241] The original text uses the term 'ishuyori'. An exhaustive consultation of this word in most dictionaries in Assamese, Bengali and its dialects, and in Persian did not produce any result. A printing mistake may have caused the misspelling of 'ashuyori', which signifies summer rice (*ashu*) and land tax (*wary*: Source: Shakespeare, John. *A Dictionary, Hindustani and English*. 1834, p. 1831). This term perfectly fit into the scenario of the ongoing contention between the raja of Bijni and his subjects. The raja had begun to collect cash rent from other crop lands, such as summer rice or Ashu land apart from the existing winter crop lands. (For further details, see, A.J. Laine, *An Account of the Land Tenure System of Goalpara with criticisms of the existing rent law and suggestions for its amendment*, Shillong: Assam Secretariat Printing Office, 1917, p. 136.)

[242] *Jalkar.*

[243] *Bankar.*

[244] *Thalagat/Thalajat.*

[245] *Gorkati.*

[246] *Kacha charai.*

[247] *Nayeb* and *Gomasta.*

[248] *Mohori.*

[249] *Tanqih nabis.*

unpaid tax accountants,[250] estimate writers[251] and revenue officers.[252] Ananda Ram formulated these rules in line with government policies and office regulations.

At the time, the parganas' area had very little land, most of which was of uncertain categorization. The cultivated lands were not estimated, and many people received land grants from the raja for special services. Those who received these grants were given tax exemptions by praying to the raja. However, there were also many who used more land than they were granted.

Ananda Ram, recognizing the problems in the system, wanted to survey the parganas again and order a new settlement. Many cultivators had overdue tax payments for several years, but the judicial process to recover these payments was too long. Therefore, Ananda Ram suggested introducing a direct attachment of the defaulter's property against the unpaid tax. However, the people of the parganas strongly opposed this move. Local government officials attempted to persuade both parties to agree to a new, equitable settlement, but neither party was willing to compromise. Both wanted to retain the existing rent system. Despite his efforts, Ananda Ram failed to find a solution. A case was filed at the offices of the collector of Goalpara and the commissioner of Assam.

---

[250] *Jama-nabis.*

[251] *Sumar nabis.*

[252] *Tahsildar.*

Although the raja's side executed Ananda Ram's regulations, the main issue of contention between the raja and his tenants still needed to be resolved. Ananda Ram returned to Guwahati from Goalpara and submitted an application to the office of the collector and the commissioner, using both English and the court language,[253] where he presented his arguments and the legal provisions.

In October 1850, assistant sub-commissioner, Strong,[254] applied for a four-month leave from his post in Nagaon. On 4 September, in letter no. 255, the commissioner wrote to the government, recommending Ananda Ram as a temporary replacement. He mentioned that Ananda Ram was currently serving as the dewan of Bijni and had previously passed a test. The commissioner suggested that J.D. Bruce should be appointed if Ananda Ram refused the job. On 19 October, the government appointed Ananda Ram as the acting sub-assistant by order number 1826. After receiving Jenkins's letter no. 331 with the government's appointment, Ananda Ram accepted the position. Strong's leave was granted from 10 November, and Ananda Ram took charge on 11 November, travelling by a racing boat to Nagaon. As the chief assistant commissioner, Butler[255] had to leave for the Naga Hills, and Ananda Ram took

---

[253] The court language referred to here was Bengali incorporated with many Persian terms.

[254] C.R. Strong.

[255] John Butler.

charge of the treasury and daily affairs. Even though he was stationed at the circuit house, he constructed a few cottages nearby, where he ate and slept and used the bungalow only for his study. His sister came from Jakhalabandha Satra to stay with him for a few days. Although this was his first posting, Ananda Ram managed his work quite easily. He also managed the affairs of the Bijni raja as much as possible from such a distance. Butler returned at the beginning of January and took back the district's charge from Ananda Ram. Ananda Ram successfully completed his tenure of three months, met with several relatives and acquaintances, and returned to Guwahati. His sister and her son Chandrahas accompanied him.

Ananda Ram moved to Goalpara to replace sub-assistant Driver, who was on medical leave. At the same time, a survey was being conducted at Jamira Pargana. A scuffle broke out between the villagers and some workers from the survey department, and a case was filed. Ananda Ram was sent to investigate the matter, and after completing his inquiry, he submitted a report to the magistrate.

Later, a huge dispute arose between Pratap Chandra Barua, the zamindar of Rangamati and the tenants of Ghulla Pargana, who opposed the settlement. Ananda Ram was ordered to investigate the conflict. Accompanied by a police officer named Imtazuddin and a clerk named Shyamacharan Mukujje, Ananda Ram went to Kaltoba, where the dispute had occurred. He returned to Goalpara after completing the inquiry and handed over the charge to Driver upon his return. Later, he completed a few assignments for the Bijni raja and returned to Guwahati in the month of Bohag.[256]

During those days, most of the rulings made by the highest civil and criminal courts[257] were printed in English, with the government's support, and made available to the courts and public every month. However, it was challenging for the average person to comprehend the orders and opinions of higher court judges since the documents were not in Bengali. Ananda Ram recognized this gap and wanted to publish the highest civil court's judgments in Bengali. He came up with this idea while he was serving in Nagaon. From January 1850, he started translating the monthly decrees and sent them to the Rozario Company in Calcutta for printing. The first judgment collections that were printed were those of January and February. This was the first-ever selection of court orders in Bengali. Although many such collections are available now, Ananda Ram's ingenuity and vision had led to this idea.

During the month of Puh,[258] Balaram Phukan's mother passed away while Ananda Ram was still in Nagaon. After Ananda Ram returned in the month of Bohag, Balaram's wife, Bishnupriya, also passed away, leaving behind a daughter named Navadurga. During that same month, an epidemic broke out in Guwahati, and Gangaram succumbed

---

[256] April–May.

[257] The Sudder Dewani criminal courts of the East India Company government in Calcutta.

[258] December–January.

to it. Shortly thereafter, Balaram fell ill with a severe fever. All these events left Ananda Ram feeling despondent.

In the conflict related to surveying, settlement and remittance of unpaid revenue, the local administrators failed to deliver the desired result for Ananda Ram. Both the Goalpara collector and the commissioner of Assam ruled against the raja's interests. As a result, Ananda Ram filed an appeal to the Sudder Board of Revenue in Calcutta. The nature of the appeal was very grave, being against the ruling of local bureaucrats. Seeking advice from the many learned lawyers and counsels in Calcutta seemed to be the best option for a favourable outcome. Taking all these factors into account, Ananda Ram decided to visit Calcutta with the raja's approval. Both the commissioner and his deputy also advised him to do so.

Calcutta is a magnificent city, and Ananda Ram was eager to go there. Gunabhiram was studying in the first class in Guwahati and was still adored by Ananda Ram just as before. He had previously worked as a substitute teacher at Guwahati Seminary when a teacher was unavailable. However, his financial situation had worsened, and Gunabhiram hoped to become an apprentice in the collectorate. Ananda Ram, who was leaving for Calcutta, advised Gunabhiram to come along, and he agreed. Ananda Ram told him that he could become a sub-assistant by studying in Calcutta.

In those days, a government steamer would occasionally stop in Guwahati, with Major Bruce[259] serving as the

---

[259] C.A. Bruce.

steamer agent. He was accused of stealing parcels sent on the steamer. The trial was presided over by Dalton, the magistrate of Guwahati, with the help of a jury. During the trial, the magistrate did not appoint the usual assisting jurors. However, seven jurors, including Ananda Ram and Jagat Chandra Mukujje, were chosen to assist with the trial. After the trial, the jury declared the accused guilty, and the magistrate forwarded the case file, along with the jury members' decision, to the deputy commissioner. As a result, Bruce was convicted.

One day, Reverend Bland met Gunabhiram during his morning walk while the trial was still ongoing. The reverend asked Gunabhiram to remind Ananda Ram to treat others the way he wanted to be treated.

All the necessary preparations for the journey had been completed. The boat was finalized, and the luggage was loaded on board. Ananda Ram was accompanied by his travel team, which included Gunabhiram, Ramnath, a Brahmin named Birdatta from the pargana, two servants named Puwaram and Balaram, a Bengali named Prasanna Kumar Ray and his servant Birohu, also known as Tepuram. Shambhu was also planning to travel with them but left midway. On the afternoon of 4 September 1851, the boat set sail from Guwahati, and they stopped at Khanamukh the same day. Khanamukh is known for its health benefits. Balaram Phukan used to come here to breathe the fresh air and improve his health. From here, one can get a clear view of Guwahati. The British often visit this place to enjoy its clean air. It is also the site where the Ahom army defeated Muslim invaders with their innovative tactics.

The next day, they set sail and arrived in Goalpara at five in the evening. Ananda Ram changed their boat and consulted with Bijni officials for two days before resuming the journey. At Berarkona, near Sirajganj, one of the boatmen was replaced. Before Ananda Ram set off for Calcutta, he prepared a set of Assamese-style attire, which included a turban, long robes and a silk dhoti with no pleats. When he disembarked at Sirajganj in this attire, people assumed he was either a south Indian or a Marwari. During the next day's sailing on the Jamuna River, the boat got stuck in shallow water several times. At one point, it was about to capsize after getting stuck in quicksand, but the passengers, especially Devasingha, who had boarded the boat in Goalpara, managed to save it. The boat sailed through the Jamuna, Hurasagar, the Chalan Kalan wetland and the Baral River before reaching the mouth of the river at Sardah.

The Chalan wetland is a vast area where one can head to Dinajpur by moving north-eastwards or to the river's mouth at Sardah by moving north-west. There are many highlands scattered along the wetland, and they have villages, buildings and marketplaces. During the winter season, one can walk from one highland to another. At Sardah, there is an indigo storage and another jute storage. Beggars with a bag floating on a wide-mouthed earthen pot come to beg from the boats.

The Padma River flowing through Sardah is vast and has a powerful current, making it risky to cross by boat. To mitigate this risk, people typically hire a pilot boat with two boatmen to lead the way. The team hired a pilot boat for one rupee and set sail in the morning. By 9 a.m., they reached Kharia, a distributary of the Padma River. A downstream sail followed through Kharia, and they arrived at Gowari Krishnanagar. At this point, taxes were collected from cargo boats based on their weight and from passenger boats based on the number of oars. Additionally, boat inspections were conducted to look for taxable items. After paying the taxes, Ananda Ram went sightseeing in Krishnanagar, a significant town in Nadia district.

The following day, the boat arrived at the Ganga, a relatively narrow river. At noon, it docked at Kalna in Bardhaman district, where a grand royal temple of Goddess Ambika was located. After visiting the temple, Ananda Ram and the boat sailed downstream towards Santipur. The boat was anchored at Boyra moorage, as Ananda Ram had planned to visit Parbatiya Gosain's village. He took a palanquin to Shimla village, the ancestral home of the Gosains. However, they were not known as Parbatiya Gosain in the village; instead, they were famous as the Assamese Bhattacharjya. Ananda Ram was a disciple of Kalidas Bhattacharjya, who belonged to that family. Ananda Ram was overjoyed to meet his guru and returned to the boat after having lunch there. The Bhattacharjya house resembled other houses in the village, and their status was no different from that of the other Brahmins; they did not command the same awe and respect they received in our country.

The Ganga experiences higher tides on certain special days as it flows towards the sea. In Santipur, the water level rises to around two inches[260] during high tide. The boat started from Boyra's mooring and sailed through Ula and Guptipara, passing by Sukhchar, Banshberia, Hooghly, Noihati, Chandannagar, Srirampore, Barakpore, Panihati and Agarpara situated on both sides of the river. After spending the night at Ghusuri, the boat reached Calcutta at 8 a.m. As usual, Calcutta was filled with water everywhere. Ananda Ram got off the boat with Devasingha at Mirbah Ghat[261] and went to the city on a palanquin. He directed the boat to dock at the Chandpal ghat.

Ananda Ram went to visit his friend Shyamcharan Das at his home in Potuatola. Shyamcharan's entire family was delighted to meet Ananda Ram, and his house became a temporary abode for the visitors. After unloading, Ananda Ram released the boat. The entire journey had taken eighteen days. He stayed at Shyamcharan's house for two days before moving to an old Boithakkhana alley. However, as this house was unsuitable, they relocated to an excellent single-storey building at No. 12, Panchanantola Alley, near College Square. Ananda Ram chose this house because it

---

[260] *Chari Angul*: height/length estimation by four-finger scaling.

[261] Mooring spot on a riverbank.

was located in a peaceful area and was close to his friends'
residences.

Ananda Ram was occupied with the king's duties for
several days. Since the rates for rental cars were high, he
bought a buggy and a horse, hiring a coachman to drive
it. Unfortunately, Puwaram and Devasingha passed away
from cholera. Ananda Ram employed Advaita, a Bengali
servant, and a Hindustani watchman. In Calcutta, it was
common for aristocratic families to have a watchman who
acted as both a doorman and a security guard. Additionally,
since Prasanna Kumar had to leave, Ananda Ram hired
Nimai Chatujje as a clerk-shopper to purchase various
items in Calcutta.

Chapter 4

Ananda Ram was promptly occupied with the assignment from the Bijni raja. He applied to the provincial government after the Sudder Board of Revenue[262] did not yield a favourable result. When he still did not receive a positive reply from the provincial authority, he grew concerned. The raja's mukhtars, Jay Shankar and Bhavani Shankar, were deeply disappointed. On behalf of the tenants, Premnarayan Dewan announced the victory of the tenants and the raja's loss from Calcutta. The raja became extremely forlorn and wrote to Ananda Ram, urging him to find a way somehow. He had already promised to permanently grant a duwar named Dirma in Hawraghat and offer Ananda Ram a cash reward. However, Ananda Ram was disappointed, as he had come in person yet had not managed to deliver.

In Calcutta, a member of the elite class named Prasanna Tagore worked as a lawyer in the Sudder civil court. Tagore, an acquaintance of Ananda Ram's, had helped him with an application that Ananda Ram intended to submit to

---

[262] Chief Board of Revenue of the East India Company government in Calcutta.

the Indian government. The application, addressed to Major Halliday, secretary of the Government of India, requested that the government sanction the settlement of Bijni. Upon going through Ananda Ram's submission, the secretary directed the provincial government to reconsider the raja's prayer. However, the Bengal government took no significant action beyond directing the Sudder Revenue Board to review the proposal.

The board deliberated extensively on the proposal. Ananda Ram presented his arguments both verbally and in writing to the board members—which included Currie[263] sahab, Gordon[264] sahab, Ricketts[265] sahab and its secretary, Bidwell[266] sahab—highlighting the relationship between the raja and his subject and urging the government to take steps to ensure justice was done. Ananda Ram cited a similar incident during Scott's tenure as commissioner when a settlement had been arranged. The board responded that resolving the matter would require a highly paid gazetted or non-gazetted officer, along with many employees, and would cost around Rs 50,000. Moreover, they believed such a settlement offered little hope of advancing the raja's cause.

---

[263] Edward Currie, a member and a former secretary of the Board, was Special Commissioner of Bengal in 1847.

[264] Evelyn Meadows Gordon, former Commissioner of Revenue of Dacca, was appointed at Sadr Board of Revenue, Calcutta in June 1847.

[265] Henry Ricketts.

[266] Alfred Clarke Bidwell.

Consequently, they decided to seek the commissioner's opinion and wrote to him. This decision gave a glimmer of hope to Ananda Ram, who had submitted several applications to the board and the government. He also held multiple meetings with the board members, the board secretary and the government secretary, during which he discussed various topics concerning Assam, besides the raja's case. These interactions gave the Europeans a better understanding of affairs in Assam. Previously, they had only received news from local officials and appeals in some cases. Such topics were also not reported before by any native to such high-ranking officials.

In 1850, Ananda Ram printed the selections of the Sudder civil court judgments for January and February at the Rozario Press. However, he faced some difficulties and had only been able to publish the March volume at the Baptist Mission Press. By 1852, it was too late to print any selections from 1850, so he decided to print the decrees from January 1852. He began translating the orders and nominated his friend, Nabin Chandra Ray—a writer clerk at the Military Accountant Office—as the agent of this selection. However, Ananda Ram knew that without the government's help, this major initiative would be impossible, and popular acceptance would be difficult to obtain.

Moreover, printing needed a lot of capital investment, and there was no guarantee that subscribers would regularly pay their dues to back this project. Consequently, Ananda Ram applied to the Sudder court for assistance, but the judges decided that Bengali translations of the decrees would not be of much utility. Instead of translating all the orders, it would be sufficient if Ananda Ram translated the indexes, the court added. Initially, the judges were sceptical about how an Assamese individual could manage and circulate the Bengali translations of the decrees, but Ananda Ram allayed their concerns by showing them his translations and how people were responding to them. Despite the discouraging words from the Sudder court, Ananda Ram pledged to print these translations as long as he was getting public support.

While staying in Calcutta, Ananda Ram arranged a bed on the floor in one room and a table with chairs in another, just like at home. He kept in touch with his friends, including Shyamacharan Das, Nabin Chandra Ray and Sitanath Ghosh, through regular conversations held at his residence. He also had his translations of decrees reviewed by a scholar. In addition, he enjoyed visiting tourist attractions and attending events across the city. In the beginning, Ananda Ram wore an Assamese silk dhoti with an *angarakha*,[267] a turban and *lopeta* shoes[268] when he went out in Calcutta. However, he felt ill at ease as this traditional attire drew too much attention. To fit in with the locals, he switched to wearing a pyjama, chapkan[269] or a *kaba*,[270] worn with an Assamese turban or a hat.

---

[267] A long tunic.

[268] A hybrid of pumps and slipper.

[269] A long coat.

[270] A calf-length loose fitting robe.

Many festivals were celebrated in Calcutta during the winter season when people from different places brought various articles or performed different kinds of shows. South of Shibpur village, across the river from Calcutta, lay an exotic garden known as the Botanical Garden or Company Garden. This garden housed plants and trees from many countries. Pathways made of broken brick, brick dust or coal led visitors through the magnificently organized trees and plants. The Female Normal School in Calcutta was a girls' school known for producing beautiful items such as handkerchiefs and caps. These were exhibited on a specific day in a particular venue, which many people visited to buy things; the profits were used for the school's development. In 1852, a fair was held at the Botanical Garden on the first of January.

Ananda Ram attended the fair with his teacher, Ramchandra Mitra, travelling by boat from Chandpal Ghat. The fair was arranged in small tents, and many Europeans and a few native gentlemen were in attendance. Ramchandra introduced Ananda Ram to several of them. However, there was a nuisance created by a drunk man. Afterwards, Ananda Ram went to Bishop College, where he explored the church, the college, the teachers' housing and the students' dormitory. There, he met Sinduram Das, a student from Assam who had remained on campus after converting to Christianity. From Bishop College, Ananda Ram travelled by boat to the memorial erected by

Governor-General Lord Ellenborough[271] to commemorate the victory in the Gwalior War. He returned to his quarters following that.

On most winter mornings, horse races were held in Calcutta at Fort Field. Riders, dressed in body-hugging suits, raced their horses from one marked point to another. The winner received a prize along with the betting amount and other valuables. Members of the Horse Racing Society and ticketholders enjoyed the event while seated in chairs arranged under a tent. The races drew large crowds, including Ananda Ram, who also attended.

Revisiting places associated with childhood memories is deeply enjoyable, and Ananda Ram was thrilled to see Hindu College, his alma mater, during this journey.

At Fort Field stood a war memorial known as the Ochterlony Monument, built to commemorate General Ochterlony's victory in the Nepal War. Nearby, an arena was set up using a thatch, along with canopies and benches for spectators. Horse racing and horse dancing were some of the sports performed within this arena, and tickets needed to be purchased to attend the event, which was called the Royal Olympic Circus. There were different seating classes for the spectators, and Ananda Ram watched the circus on a Rs 4 ticket. It was a spectacular show. Men in tight-fitting costumes rode horses and ran around the arena. A woman danced and played with a sword while standing

---

[271] Edward Law Ellenborough, Governor-General of India, during 1842–1844.

on a racehorse. There was also a pony that danced, stood
up, lay down and performed many other acts taking cues
from a man.

The Council of the Governor General had a member
named Bethune.[272] He had played a significant role in
promoting education, especially among women and
established a school for women using his own funds. In his
honour, a committee known as the Bethune Society was
formed by European and native gentlemen. In January 1852,
Ananda Ram attended the society's inaugural meeting.
During the gathering, general rules were established, and
Dr Surjo Kumar Chakraborty[273] delivered an essay on
public hygiene in Calcutta. It addressed various themes,
including water supply, air quality, sewage management
and housing conditions. Dr Chakraborty also proposed
that Indians should adopt European attire, a suggestion
that met with opposition from many members. Dr Mouat,
the president of this meeting, also opposed this proposition.
The society—which included many notable people such as
Major Marshall,[274] Ramchandra Mitra and Ram Gopal

---

[272] John Elliot Drinkwater Bethune (d. 1851), a mathematician and
polyglot, founded one of the oldest girls' schools in Asia in Calcutta
in 1849. He came to India after being appointed as a law member in
the Council of the Governor-General of the East India Company
government.

[273] Dr Soorjo Coomar Goodeve Chuckerbutty (d. 1874) of the
Indian Medical Service was a professor of Calcutta Medical College.

[274] Major G.T. Marshall.

Ghosh[275]—assembled on a Thursday evening every month.
Ananda Ram became a regular member. At that time, Dr
Mouat was still the president, and Pyari Chand Mitra[276]
served as secretary. Dr Mouat requested Ananda Ram to
write an essay on any subject related to Assam.

In Calcutta, a grand two-storey building known as the
Town Hall served as the venue for important events and
functions. On 14 January, Ananda Ram attended an award
ceremony for students graduating from Hindu College,
Madrasa College and Sanskrit College. The event drew
many European and native gentlemen, including Pratap
Sinha, Raja Kalikrishna, Krishnamohan Bandopadhyay
and Kumar Jalaluddin. The deputy governor of Bengal
arrived at noon and, following the distribution of awards,
delivered a speech. The ceremony concluded with his
address. Afterwards, Ananda Ram explored the upper
storey of the building. On the second floor were portraits
of Napoleon Bonaparte, W. Bird,[277] Mr Cameron,[278] Sir
Edward Ryan[279] and Dwarakanath, as well as a magnificent
portrait of Queen Victoria.

There were two factories near Calcutta—one
for producing yarn and the other for making paper.

---

[275] Ram Gopal Ghosh established and edited a bilingual perodical
called, The Bengal Spectator in 1842.

[276] Peary Chand Mitra was a writer, cultural activist and entrepreneur.

[277] W.W. Bird was the deputy Governor of Bengal.

[278] Charles Hay Cameron was the president of the Council of
Education, Bengal.

[279] He was the chief justice of the Supreme Court at Calcutta.

Ananda Ram visited both with Ramchandra Mitra and was thrilled by the quick production of yarn and paper. Calcutta also had a mint[280] that produced coins of different denominations, including one rupee, half, quarter, one-eighth and one-sixteenth rupee coins. Bangshidhar Sen, the dewan or chief executive of the mint and a former batchmate of Ananda Ram's, gave him a tour of the facility. Ananda Ram learnt about the coin-making process. It began with melting the metals, which were then shaped into a mould as large as a sheet and then flattened. This sheet was then moulded into round coins of different values. The edges of these coins were shaped using a machine. In the last step, the coins were pressed and stamped with their respective designs in a tunnel-like machine. Finally, workers collected and sorted the finished coins. The mint produced coins worth Rs 3–3.5 lakh each day.

Motilal Seal, a wealthy resident of Calcutta, had a son who studied at Hindu College. After the boy was caned by a teacher, Motilal decided to establish his own school, which he named Seal College. Ananda Ram attended the college's annual award ceremony.

On certain evenings, Professor Liz [sic][281] performed alongside his two sons. The boys would dance on top of their father's head, and with a gentle touch of his finger, they

---

[280] The Calcutta Mint was established in 1757 by the East India Company under a treaty with the Nawab of Bengal.

[281] V. L. Rees was a Professor of Mathematics at Hindu College.

would fall into a deep sleep. With another touch, they would make different sounds. They could also pause and remain still like statues. One night, Ananda Ram attended their performance, and on another day, he went to Bali Uttarpara with Ramchandra to see a railway construction site. The track was laid with wooden sleepers and a foundation of broken bricks. He also visited a shipbuilding dock at Bally canal and a winery owned by a French businessman. Afterwards, he went to see the Shiv temple established by Rani Rashmoni before returning to his rented residence.

At Calcutta's Medical College, European medical science was taught through two divisions. The English section used English as the medium of instruction, while the military or native section conducted lessons in Hindustani. Some students from Assam, including Dil Mohammed and Keramat Ali from Barpeta, Rahmat Ali, Majkar Hussain and Ajim Hussain from Guwahati, Bhakatram from Sivasagar, Jagyaram from Tezpur and Shivaram and Bidehi Singh from Dibrugarh, studied in the native section. The college museum had specimens of never-seen-before diseases and other fascinating items. Ananda Ram visited the museum and saw a skeleton of an animal said to be a hybrid of a camel and a tiger, the body of an old woman with no flesh and dried skin who still appeared lifelike, as well as specimens of a two-headed calf, a two-headed boy, Siamese twins, a big-headed boy and a very tiny-headed boy. There were some samples of flesh preserved in medicine. Ananda Ram also visited the Fever Hospital, located inside a tall and large building, where patients were treated for various ailments. In earlier times, Bengalis had avoided the study of medicine because they did not consider it proper to dissect dead bodies. The college gallery displayed a statue of Madhusudan Gupta, the first Bengali to perform a dissection. Ananda Ram found these encounters both astonishing and deeply fascinating.

Fort William, a citadel in Calcutta, houses both European and native military personnel. Upon entering the fort, one feels as though entering an underground structure. The fort receives water from the Ganga, through a canal running beside a bridge. It contains a large arsenal of bullets, gunpowder, guns and other weapons, with large shells stored in heaps outside. The long concrete barracks serve as accommodation for the soldiers. The fort, which stores army uniforms, has a church and six gates for carriages and horses to pass through. Ananda Ram was shown around the fort by his friend Gobinda Chandra Sen, the supervisor. Lord Clive had constructed the fort around 130 years ago, at a cost of approximately Rs 2 crore.

At a building, known as the Asiatic Museum, various ancient and modern items were on display, including silver and gold dust, stuffed birds, animals, a lion, a tiger and many old and new books. Ananda Ram visited the museum and conversed with the learned Bengali librarian, Rajendra Lal Mitra. On one occasion, Ananda Ram went to Serampore on a boat with Ramchandra and a few other Assamese men, including Gunabhiram. There, he visited the printing press and paper mill. Atmaram, an Assamese Brahmin and expert in printing, had visited Serampore before the Burmese invasion. He had married, had children and settled in the area, where he assisted Pastor Dr Carey in printing the first Assamese Christian scripture, the Bible.[282] Ananda Ram also visited the Governor's House and the garden in Chanak or Barrackpore, where he saw a live lion and met his old friend, Dr Scott.[283] On another occasion, he visited the factory at Kashipur. Several wealthy people from Calcutta had built farmhouses, which they visited occasionally, in and around that place, also known as Satpukur. In that stunningly beautiful place, Shyam Mallick also owned a farmhouse that Ananda Ram visited.

Ananda Ram enjoyed attending weddings and other ceremonies organized by his friends. He was present at the wedding of his friend Shyambabu's daughter, Bindu, who married the nephew of another friend, Nabin Chandra Karmakar. In Bengali weddings, the bride is carried on a stool with her uncovered head adorned by a crown. Ananda Ram also attended the wedding ceremony of the grandson of Ashutosh Dey, also known as Chatu Babu, one of the wealthiest men in Calcutta. Many judges from the Sudder court, as well as other prominent European and native gentlemen, attended the musical programme arranged for the occasion. However, attending weddings was not the

---

[282] William Carey of British Baptist Mission published Dharmapustak, the Assamese translation of the Bible, in 1813.

[283] Most probably, Dr Scott is Dr K.M. Scott, who was posted in Guwahati earlier and donated Rs 20 during the publication of Ananda Ram's book, *Asamiya Lorar Mitra*.

only activity on Ananda Ram's agenda. He also took a dip in the Ganga on Magh Bihu and performed the Sandhya Tarpan.[284] Additionally, he visited the Kalighat Temple to pay his respects to the goddess and made donations. However, he was bothered by little girls and beggars there, though he gave alms to the poor and beggars at home.

Ananda Ram also visited the Shivalaya established by Satyacharan Ghoshal, the raja of Bhukailash in Khidirpur, where a fair was organized during Shivratri. Satyacharan, who admired Ananda Ram, fondly remembered how Ananda Ram's father, Haliram, had once called him 'brother'. Ananda Ram also enjoyed the Holi celebrations at the home of Motilal Seal, a very wealthy individual.

Ananda Ram closely observed various trials and proceedings at the Supreme Court, Sudder Civil and Criminal Courts, Alipore Court, the police office and the lower courts. He occasionally visited prominent European and native gentlemen, such as Raja Radhkanta Bahadur, Kalikrishna Bahadur, Debendra Nath Tagore, Gobinda Chandra Sen, Madhab Chandra Sen, Shibdas Dutta, Ananda Dutta, Pyari Chand Mitra and Gopikrishna Mitra. He regularly met with Motilal Seal, Nagendranath Tagore, Ramchandra Mitra, Shyamacharan Das, Nabin Chandra Karmakar, Sitanath Ghosh and Prasanna Kumar Tagore, all of whom held him in high esteem.

---

[284] A religious ceremony performed every morning, evening and noon by a Hindu.

He used to attend prayers regularly at different churches and at the Brahmo Society. Some days, he felt very grateful to God after attending prayers or other performances. In the city, Ananda Ram also visited shops owned by prominent Englishmen or others. One day, he saw a pair of bangles that cost Rs 6000. Being a tropical region, Calcutta imported ice from America, which arrived on ships in two large, white rock-like blocks. At Fort Maidan, there was a beautiful garden known as Auckland Garden or Eden Park. Gentlemen regularly visited the park in the evening, where an English band played at the same time. Ananda Ram visited the park daily. The park had been built during the tenure of Governor-General Lord Auckland.

Metcalfe Hall, a large building, has a public library that contains 16,000 books on various subjects. Ananda Ram visited the library almost every day to read and compiled a list of the books he had read. On 9 March, he felt overwhelmed after reading a biography of Peter the Great, the Russian king who had succeeded in his endeavour to improve his country. Inspired by this, Ananda Ram pledged to work even harder for Assam's development.

Calcutta is a place full of temptations, where many locals aspire to live lives of enjoyment and leisure. However, Ananda Ram never succumbed to the temptations, even though he knew a few such people and occasionally visited them. One day, a person claimed that drinking wine or having an extramarital affair was neither an offence nor a sin. He also declared that he did not follow the dictums of the scripture, which astonished Ananda Ram. He also detested the fact that some people drank alcohol in secret. He was stunned upon seeing a foreign-returned man drinking wine while eating rice with his hands.

Captain Brodie, the chief assistant of Sivasagar, visited Calcutta on his way to England, accompanied by two Assamese boys, Priyalal and Minadhar. These boys stayed near Ananda Ram's place before joining Hooghly College. Ananda Ram also helped Gunabhiram gain admission to Kolutola Branch School with the assistance of Mouat.

As the Revenue Board forwarded the papers to the commissioner, Ananda Ram decided to return, as he was no longer required to stay in Calcutta. He bought several items, including copies of the incomplete *Bhagavat*, *Kamakhya Jatra Paddhati* and *Smriti Shastra* from the book auction at the Samachar Chandrika Press. He planned to return via *Damuda*, a government steamer scheduled to sail to Assam and booked a cabin. He was asked to pay Rs 4 a day for dining with the captain of the steamer, even though he would not be taking any meals. Ananda Ram had to approach the captain, who decided that he need not pay. On 25 March 1852, Ananda Ram had a daguerreotype photograph[285] taken. Ananda Ram arranged for Gunabhiram's stay with his friend Nabin Chandra Ray and promised to bear his expenses. He also made Nabin the agent for the selected decrees and entrusted him with the responsibility of printing, among other things.

---

[285] The first photographic process, invented by Louis-Jacques-Mandé Daguerre (1787–1851).

After meeting his friends, a deeply saddened Ananda
Ram bid farewell to Calcutta. Shyamacharan Das and Nabin
Chandra Ray were his best friends, and Jatindramohan
Tagore, Sitanath Ghosh and Bangshidhar Sen were his
classmates. There were also many acquaintances whose
names he listed in his diary, including Nabin Chandra
Karmakar, Prankrishna Vidyasagar, Gobichandra Dhar,
Motilal Seal, Prasanna Kumar Tagore, Raja Radhakanta
Deb and a few Europeans, including Halliday, Mouat and
Major Marshall.

He had already sent some of his belongings with
Prasanna Kumar Ray on a boat. He boarded the ship at
noon on Friday, 26 March 1852. The steamer began its
voyage at two-thirty in the afternoon and stopped at Bazbaz
for the night. The next day, it sailed through a wider part of
the Ganga. The steamer then proceeded to the Sundarbans
via a narrow channel shrouded by date trees and jungles,
with no human habitation. They reached a village the
following day, where they collected drinking water as one
could not drink the saline water of the Sundarbans. On the
31st, they reached Khulna, a subdivision where an assistant
magistrate and a munshef were posted. Khulna had many
densely populated villages, with abundant coconut and
betel nut trees. The steamer loaded up on coal here and
then sailed to Barishal, the headquarters of Bakharganj
district. The steamer left the attached flatboat there and
sailed to Noakhali, also known as Bhulua, a subdivision of
Chattogram and Tripura district. It had a pargana named
Bhulua, an estate of Lalababu from Paikpara, whose

revenue was Rs 3 lakh. The steamer docked some distance from Noakhali, where a revenue amount of Rs 2 lakh was loaded. The steamer resumed its voyage and reached Dhaka via Barishal. In Dhaka, Ananda Ram hired a carriage and took a tour of the city. Dhaka was not an awe-inspiring and beautiful city like Calcutta. The streets were narrow and not very clean, though the city boasted huge buildings. It had an old fort where a park had been set up. At a government stable for elephants, many elephants were housed. There was a market named Chawkbazar, where a cannon was installed. The army camp was unimpressive. Dhaka's British settlement, Englishtola, was clean. The city, located on the bank of the Buriganga River, also had a college. Dhaka was a city from the old nawabi era, and the nawab himself resided there.

The following day, the steamer left Dhaka and entered the Meghna. It crossed Bikrampur and Rajnagar while sailing up the Padma and reached the Jamuna. Beautiful villages were visible on both sides of the river. The next day, on 8 April, they stopped at Sirajganj, where many boats were docked. Ananda Ram visited Barry's[286] jute warehouse there. The steamer sailed near Patiladah Pargana and reached Dhuburi after crossing Dewanganj and Jatrapur on 12 April. On the 13th, it arrived at Goalpara, where Ananda Ram had a meeting with the Bijni raja's officials, including Gouramohan Ghosh and Ramlochan Sarkar.

---

[286] G.R. Barry, a jute merchant, later owned tea gardens in Assam

They delivered the message from the raja, who placed
the responsibility entirely on Ananda Ram, claiming he
knew nothing and urged him to act for a solution. Ananda
Ram became determined to work for the raja's welfare.
The steamer left Goalpara the next day and stayed near
Duramari for the night. It reached Guwahati at 3.30 p.m.
on 15 April. During this voyage, Ananda Ram had his
meals cooked in the evenings either on the jolly boat or
on the bank. However, he had some snacks on the steamer.
He took a Shaligram to Calcutta and worshipped it every
day. On his journey back, he read many books, including
the English translation of the Quran. He had hearty
conversations with the captain, the mates and the other
passengers on the steamer.

Ananda Ram met Colonel Matthie and Major Vetch
on the steamer and they were very happy for him. Ananda
Ram then returned home on a palanquin sent to fetch him.
He was very glad to meet his mother, stepmother, wife,
daughter and other loved ones. The following day, he met
Jenkins and others. He discussed various issues related
to Bijni with the commissioner and also made written
submissions.

The marriage of Balaram Phukan, whose second wife
had passed away the previous year, was arranged with
Bhagirathi, the daughter of Krishnakingkar Goswami, who
was, in turn, the grandson of Paka Beji Duworiya. Jagyaram
Phukan had managed both households when Ananda Ram
was young. During that period, Jagyaram owed Ananda
Ram Rs 6000. Balaram agreed to pay the amount in four

annual instalments. Ananda Ram wanted half the amount immediately and the rest in instalments. However, the issue was not resolved for the time being. A few days later, Ananda Ram proposed to Balaram the idea of merging the two families again. The women from both families rejoiced at this idea. However, Ananda Ram prepared an agreement with the clause that they would divide the household and go back to the previous partition if and when they ever needed to part again. Balaram objected to this clause, and the negotiations continued. That day, they discussed the matter from two in the afternoon until eight in the evening. However, in the end, they dumped the proposal. The following day, Balaram offered to return pieces of jewellery but attached certain conditions regarding the payment. If they reached an agreement, he would pay Rs 1500 immediately, with the balance to be paid in three instalments of Rs 1500 each in 1853, 1854 and 1855.[287] Ananda Ram did not respond that day.

After retiring as the deputy commissioner, Matthie Sahab had to return to the army. As he was a very good friend, Ananda Ram was disheartened by his departure and proposed that a bust be made in Matthie's likeness, with contributions from everyone. However, his endeavour did not come to fruition.

Ananda Ram went to Goalpara on 30 April to meet the collector, Lt Agnew, and a few others. The collector

---

[287] In the original text it was 1260, 1261 and 1262 *Bangabda* or Bengali year which may be converted as 1853, 1854 and 1855, respectively.

called the raja to Goalpara, and he arrived a few days later. Lt Agnew wanted to arrange a deal between the raja and his tenants. A meeting was held at Agnew's bungalow, where the tenants presented several demands, including the abolishment of the Narayani taka rate, which was untenable for the raja. Around 150 influential tenants attended the meeting. It was clear to everyone that there was no hope for a compromise anymore. The tenants had gained more confidence, as the outcome of the appeal in Calcutta had not been satisfactory for the raja. Still, after many consultations, Ananda Ram submitted another application and informed the raja in detail about the papers sent by the Revenue Board to the commissioner.

Balaram married the daughter of Krishnakinkar Gosain in the month of Jeth,[288] and Ananda Ram travelled to Bamundi to attend the wedding. The event was held quietly, without much fanfare.

Ananda Ram continued translating and mailing the Sudder decrees, which were then printed by Nabin in Calcutta. He bought and set up his own printing press, Calcutta New Press, in Calcutta, as printing at other presses was costlier. In 1852, this press was registered with the Calcutta Police in Gunabhiram's name. Ananda Ram did not want to use his own name, and using Nabin's name was not appropriate, as he was a government servant. Ananda Ram did not use his name as the translator of the decrees; instead, Nabin's name was published.

---

[288] May–June.

The conflict between the raja of Bijni and his tenants could not be resolved. In August, Agnew, the collector of Goalpara, went to Hawraghat Pargana to break the deadlock. On behalf of the raja, Ananda Ram accompanied Agnew. The raja had a court at Dolgoma in Hawraghat. Agnew wanted to try again to resolve the dispute. However, he fully sided with the tenants, believing that the raja tortured his tenants. Before leaving for Dolgoma, Ananda Ram received a letter from Parashuram on 7 August, informing him of the passing of his daughter, Rasheswari. Devastated by the news, Ananda Ram pledged to remain devoted to God, feeling that his own death was imminent. The journey to Hawraghat did not yield any results as the tenants were firm on their original stance. Ananda Ram returned to Guwahati on 25 August, completely distraught by his daughter's death.

The commissioner was about to write his report in response to the board's queries. The collector of Goalpara also submitted a report from the ground. Ananda Ram was present at the collectorate when the commissioner wrote his report and engaged in deliberations with him that day.

From the ongoing dispute between the raja and his tenants, Ananda Ram learnt that there was no clarity on the rights of the raja and the tenants. In Bengali, which was the language of the masses, no law book was available. Therefore, Ananda Ram thought about writing a book on civil procedure, *Dewani Mokardamar Bichar Sangkranta Aainar Sara Sangraha* (A Summary of Civil Procedures), along the lines of the English book *Civil Procedure* by

MacPherson.[289] He prepared an advertisement both in English and Bengali and circulated it among the judges of the Bengal presidency for a subscription. Jenkins supported Ananda Ram a great deal in this venture.

Balaram's daughter died of cholera in August. For Ananda Ram, who was still mourning the loss of his own daughter, this news came as a bolt from the blue. After his retirement, Matthie took a ship back to Calcutta, leaving Ananda Ram deeply saddened. It was difficult for him to accept parting with a friend like Matthie, whose support had been crucial to his personal growth.

On the journey from Goalpara, Ananda Ram suffered a setback when the boat carrying his belongings, including the Bhagavad Gita from Calcutta, sank at Latuma after colliding with rocks amid strong waves. This caused him distress, especially as he was also suffering from diarrhoea, while Guwahati was at risk of an epidemic surge. Luckily, Dr Shital Singh was able to treat him. To rejuvenate himself, Ananda Ram explored Guwahati and nearby locations on elephant and boat, seeking to breathe in the fresh air.

In addition to managing the affairs of Bijni and translating the Sudder decrees, Ananda Ram received an offer for a new position on 25 September 1852. Jenkins informed him of a vacancy for an assistant commissioner and requested a meeting. During their meeting, Jenkins

---

[289] William Macpherson's *The Procedure of the Civil Courts of the East India Company: In the Presidency of Fort William, in Regular Suits* was published in 1850.

offered Ananda Ram the job in Barpeta, as the current assistant commissioner, Hudson,[290] had been transferred to Guwahati as a junior assistant. Ananda Ram happily accepted the offer, and Jenkins subsequently wrote to the government about it.

As Ananda Ram was still the dewan of Bijni, he decided to meet the raja and went to Goalpara at the end of September. Before that, Balaram had also gone to Goalpara, and the two met there. Balaram was owed a payment from the Bijni raja. He suggested that he would pay an advance of Rs 1300 out of the total sum of Rs 6000 due and return the ornaments.[291] Ananda Ram was satisfied. It was decided that Ananda Ram's mother and stepmother would accompany Balaram, who was travelling to Kashi.

Ananda Ram wanted to appoint Ramchandra Biswas, his mukhtar for many years and also a mukhtar of the Bijni Raja, as the peshkar, or record-keeper, of Bijni. Ananda Ram went to Bijni at the beginning of October, updated the raja on all developments, and Ramchandra was appointed as the new peshkar. He also submitted his accounts to the raja.

Ananda Ram arrived in Barpeta on 8 October after travelling from Goalpara. On the ninth, he took over the sub-assistant's post from Hudson. The following day, he inspected the jail and assumed other responsibilities. Hudson left for Guwahati the next day, and Ananda Ram

---

[290] C. K. Hudson.

[291] The ornaments Jagyaram and his family owed to Ananda Ram's family as the settlement between these two families.

moved into his bungalow. He constructed several buildings on the campus for dining and living quarters. Due to his previous experience in this position and similar work, Ananda Ram had little difficulty fulfilling his duties.

Ramchandra Biswas arrived in Barpeta after a few days. Ananda Ram provided him with sufficient counsel on Bijni and briefed him about the regulations and the declaration he had prepared. On 27 October, Ananda Ram's mother, wife and others arrived in Barpeta. On the same day, he received a letter from Jenkins informing him of the government's approval of his appointment. He was grateful and thanked God. On 2 November, his mother and stepmother, along with Balaram, who was still in Goalpara, began their scheduled pilgrimage to Gaya, Ganga, Kashi and Prayag. Mahindri, Ananda Ram's wife, had now become the primary decision-maker of the household. She was literate, read both Bengali and Assamese books, had basic knowledge of mathematics and kept the household accounts, along with being skilled in weaving and other crafts. Ananda Ram was content with his blissful married life.

Chapter 5

On 27 October 1852, the day his wife and mother went to
Barpeta, Ananda Ram received the gazette notification of
the government approval of his appointment, issued on 14
October 1852. He also received personal and official letters
from Jenkins. He was delighted and grateful to God. His
monthly salary was fixed at Rs 250. Jenkins was pleased
with Ananda Ram getting a permanent position. Colonel
Matthie, who was in Barrackpore, wrote a letter expressing
his happiness at the progress Ananda Ram had made: 'I am
very delighted by your growth. Look, if you had not gone
to Calcutta as Jenkins and I advised, and had not studied
well there, you would have remained without any money
and respect. Now you have the highest position among
all the Assamese and Bengali employees, and you are
the first to receive such a high post and salary. You must
show your gratitude to Jenkins through your character and
the execution of duties. You must remain grateful to the
government. Please show respect while talking to native
aristocrats. While dealing with the poor and announcing

their conviction, please forgive them for their ignorance.'
An overwhelmed Ananda Ram wrote a letter to Matthie.

After his appointment, Ananda Ram had the power
to impose a maximum sentence of six months and a fine
of Rs 200 under Assam Kaydabandi. Shortly thereafter,
he obtained the powers of a deputy collector under Law 9
of 1833.[292] While most people in our country rejoiced at
his appointment, a few were unhappy. This small section
would not have been offended if Ananda Ram had been
appointed as a munshef or a sadar amin. But he had been
appointed as a sub-assistant commissioner—a post reserved
for the English or Eurasians until then. Common people
addressed a sub-assistant commissioner as 'chota sahab',
and chief assistants as '*bor* sahab' or 'junior sahab'. While
meeting these officers, natives of all classes had to leave
their shoes outside the room and remain standing before
them after making long salutes. Even native magistrates
had to follow the ritual of taking off their shoes outside
and often made extended salutations. After Ananda Ram
became 'chota sahab', those natives who used to salute and
show reverence to foreigners were worried to death at the
thought of treating him, a native high-ranking officer, in the
same way. When a native English chota sahab in a district
in Upper Assam informed a superintendent[293] about his
transfer, adding that Ananda Ram would be joining as
the chota sahab, the superintendent allegedly exclaimed,

---

[292] Law 9 refers to The Charter Act of 1833.

[293] Sheristadar.

'My Lord! I'd better resign if Phookan sits in this chair.'
Even those jealous of his growth had to acknowledge his
superiority after learning of his vast knowledge and good
manners. One Black Anglo-Indian clerk told a native that
the chota sahab's post had lost all its glory after a Black
Indian attained that rank. However, high-ranking British
and native officials and commoners were all pleased by
Ananda Ram's elevation.

In a letter to Ananda Ram, after he was appointed
the sub-assistant commissioner, Jenkins asked him not to
be involved with Bijni in any capacity, and Ananda Ram
complied. Many people could not tolerate Ramchandra,
Ananda Ram's mukhtar, becoming the peshkar of Bijni.
Many wanted the dewan's position, which had been held
by Ananda Ram, and they reported to Agnew that Ananda
Ram was secretly acting on behalf of Bijni. Agnew submitted
an official report on the matter to the commissioner. The
commissioner then informed Ananda Ram and asked him
to quit all open and furtive relations with the raja of Bijni.
Ananda Ram replied that he had already let go of the raja's
affairs and had submitted his accounts as well.

Barpeta is an ancient site. According to the Vaishnav
saints, Lord Krishna stopped his chariot and rested here
on his way to the town of Kundil to marry Rukmini. He
stopped his chariot again on his return journey to Dwaraka
with Rukmini. These saints believe that Lord Krishna
prophesied that Barpeta would remain a holy site even
in the Age of Kali. Barpeta is also known as Chunpora,
or 'the land where the limestone powder spilled'. It is

said that Bedanidhi[294] was chewing betel nuts on Lord
Krishna's speeding chariot and might have spilled some
limestone powder juice here, hence the name. It is also said
that Sankardev[295] and Madhavdev,[296] after facing royal
oppression, moved from Upper Assam to Kamrup with
their disciples and began preaching there. Sankardev settled
in Patbausi. Damodardev's monastery was located adjacent
to Sankardev's, while Madhavdev stayed in Ganakkuchi for
seventeen years, in Sundaridiya for fourteen years and in
Barpeta for only six months. Still, Barpeta became the most
prominent among them due to its rich past.

Madhavdev paved the way for a kind of democracy
in the Barpeta Satra.[297] All the *bhakats*[298] were owners of
the Barpeta Satra. The Ahom kings also recognized this
democratic setup and granted them land. Madhavdev
nominated Mathuradas as his religious successor.
Mathuradas, in turn, delegated religious authority to
the bhakats of the Satra. They collectively selected the

---

[294] Bedanidhi played a crucial role in the marriage of Srikrishna and
Rukmini by carrying a letter from the latter to Srikrishna.

[295] Sankardev was the preeminent fifteenth- to sixteenth- century
saint-scholar and socio-religious reformer of Assam's Bhakti
movement.

[296] Sankardev's chief disciple, and a distinguished scholar of Bhakti
literature.

[297] Vaishnav monastery.

[298] A bhakat is a Vaishnav disciple living in a satra.

satriya,[299] who served as the president of the bhakat collective. The descendants of Sankardev's priest Ramaram used to be nominated as the satriya. As the satriya had been nominated from the same family for many years, the family had started to consider the post their monopoly and saw themselves as the owners of the bhakats. This attempt to usurp their rights[300] led to animosity between the satriya and the bhakats. Many legal cases were filed. In addition to the residents of Satra, people living outside the area also started to take sides.

Ananda Ram learnt the details after visiting various Satras, including Barpeta, Ganakkuchi, Patbausi, Baradi and Sundaridiya. Once, he had to sit inside the entrance area to inquire into a clash that had erupted among the Satriyas. At that point, it was impossible to know which side would be going to fight with the opposite party or when. On another day, Ananda Ram learnt about scuffling while he was at home. He went to the Satra but returned from the gate without intervening.

In January 1853,[301] a Sunday and a new-moon day, Mahindri delivered a baby girl. She was given the concealed name Pholguprabha and the public name Lakshmi in

---

[299] The head of a Vaishnav monastery.

[300] Ramaram's descendants believed that the Satriya position was reserved exclusively for their family and they were unhappy as the collective proposed for a Satriya from outside their family.

[301] In the original text, the date is 17 Puh, 1774 Sak, which may be converted as 9 January 1853 CE.

her horoscope. At the time, a story titled 'Padmavati' was published in a monthly magazine in Calcutta. Ananda Ram liked the name and thus chose Padmavati for his daughter. Having recently lost a child, he showered his newborn with love.

Barpeta is a sub-division of Kamrup district and is sparsely populated. Although its people were widely known to be very notorious, Ananda Ram, during his term, did not find this stereotype to be true. The residents were highly conscious of their rights. One munshef was posted there, and Ananda Ram occasionally conversed with a few local gentlemen. Religious preachers from the Satra and other places, as well as other gentlemen, would visit him. Sometimes, Atiram Barua[302] from Sundaridiya, as well as Hariprasad Choudhury and Gangaprasad Chakrabarty, who had worked at Hadirachoki during Brahmachari's time, visited him. Ananda Ram relished their stories on diverse themes.

Ananda Ram assigned Nabin the task of selecting decrees from the Sudder Diwani Court.[303] Nabin and Prasanna Ghosh printed and published the selected decrees at the New Press. Ananda Ram once considered translating Macpherson's *Civil Procedure* but eventually abandoned the idea. When he wrote a report on the recovery process of revenue arrears from defaulting farmers by choudhurys and

---

[302] See Chapter 2.

[303] The highest court of civil and revenue matters of the East India Company government in Calcutta.

mouzadars, he did not refer to existing legal regulations. Later, he aspired to write a treatise on Bengal's judicial system similar to Blackstone's[304] *Commentaries on the Laws of England.* He began researching all applicable government laws and regulations, including British laws for Hindus and Muslims. He had enough spare time in Barpeta to work on this project. After going through these books, he started translating them into Bengali. As Hariprasad's son, Gobindaram, had good handwriting, so he was tasked with copying the translation.

When Padmavati was four or five months old, Mahindri suffered from seizures and remained unconscious for a few days. She was eventually treated by Dr Daya Singh, who arrived from Goalpara, and she recovered by the grace of God. At the time, Ananda Ram wanted to take her to Goalpara for treatment and wrote a letter to the commissioner asking for his transfer.

After the British takeover of Assam, officials sent or appointed by the British ruled the region. No high-ranking British official ever visited to assess the situation. However, the government sent Mills,[305] a judge of the Sudder Court, to Assam to report on the issues of the region. Ananda Ram was knowledgeable about Assam and learnt about the issues that needed to be investigated by talking to officers and other gentlemen in Calcutta.

---

[304] William Blackstone, the English jurist known for his *Commentaries on the Laws of England.*

[305] A.J. Moffatt Mills.

Initially, Ananda Ram considered submitting an application on behalf of the people and drafted it in English. However, he later realized that he should not submit an application on behalf of everyone. Instead, he composed a lengthy essay—a memorandum of sorts— listing various grievances and matters the government had long neglected. The memorandum addressed wide-ranging concerns, including land rights, land settlement, permanent settlement, waste or forest land, the civil, criminal and revenue judicial systems, oaths, language and language teaching, schools and school education, agriculture, commerce, the arts and looming epidemics that could affect both humans and animals. He also covered policing, law and order and marriage registration. The memorandum was filled with logical arguments.

Mills sailed upstream from Guwahati. Eager to present his memorandum in person, Ananda Ram applied for fifteen-day leave, which was granted. However, he was required to move to Nagaon, as Strong, the sub-assistant commissioner of Nagaon, had passed away. His mother and stepmother had returned to Barpeta from their pilgrimage to Gaya. Ananda Ram thought that sailing with his family members would be cumbersome and instead sent them ahead by boat. His household had around forty members. He had already bought the Chandkuchi farm from the Baruas of Chandkuchi, the Mazar Khat farm, a rent-free land,[306] and the Beharbari farm from the Nagosain family.

---

[306] Brahmottar.

The paddy produced at the Kharadhara farm relieved his burden. During that period, things were not that expensive.

Driver was appointed as Ananda Ram's replacement in Barpeta. Ananda Ram handed over charge to Driver on 19 June. As was customary, clerks and locals sought certificates from Ananda Ram before his departure, and he issued many. The number of visitors was so high that he spoke with them until midnight. He began his journey the following day.

His first stop was the Satra in Baniyakuchi village, Sarukhetri Pargana, where he met with the Gosains,[307] who were Brahmins and long-time friends of the Phukan family. The family's servants and maids were disciples of the Gosain of Baniyakuchi. After visiting the Gosains, Ananda Ram travelled the next day to see the boats carrying his family near Hajo.

They spent the night near Dolibari Pasaria and reached Guwahati through the Hajo *suti*[308] the next morning. In Guwahati, he met with Jenkins and others, and later went to meet Mills, who arrived by ship on 4 July. Ananda Ram personally submitted his memorandum to Mills, who accepted it gladly and asked him further questions about the region. Ananda Ram provided all the information he could. Mills included the memorandum in his official report to the government, and it was later printed as an

---

[307] Heads of the satras.

[308] A distributary or a small branch of a river.

appendix to the report.[309] Mills agreed with Ananda Ram that the Assamese language ought to be be used in Assam and incorporated other issues raised by Ananda Ram. Ananda Ram's input was very effective, as he had foretold many things that are now being implemented. That memorandum could well be published as a book.

Balaram was on a pilgrimage when his house caught fire, resulting in significant losses. Meanwhile, Ananda Ram was in Barpeta. The two Phukans, who had been feuding, finally ended their animosity by striking a deal in which the junior Phukan agreed to repay the sum he owed Ananda Ram. After settling his accounts with the junior Phukan and inspecting his estates in Guwahati, Ananda Ram began his journey to Nagaon. He also took the opportunity to reconnect with some old friends. Ananda Ram purchased the bungalow where Strong used to stay, from Barrack Master Martin for Rs 1000, but it did not have enough space for his entire family. So, he left them in Guwahati and sailed alone on a racing boat on 14 July. The route from Guwahati to Laumudoi Ghat along the Kolong River had few farms and no visible villages. Between Jagi and Machkhowa, the riverbanks were sparsely populated. As he continued upstream through Killing, he passed only two riverside villages—Dharamtul and Ahatguri. He eventually reached Raha, crossing near the Chaparmukh weekly market. From Raha, he sailed once again on the

---

[309] A.J. Moffatt Mills' detailed report titled "Report on the Province of Assam" was published in 1854.

Kolong, which had Tiwa[310] villages on both sides. Ananda
Ram enjoyed the serene countryside landscape and arrived
in Nagaon on 19 July. He took charge of his duties from
Captain Butler, the chief assistant commissioner of
Nagaon district.

Ananda Ram was thrilled to return to Nagaon, a place
with which he was already familiar. Along with a few aides,
he stayed at the bungalow he had purchased from Strong
and began renovations, as it was insufficient for his large
family. Strong's outhouses could be used only as stables
or for outdoor activities. The bungalow was suitable for
sitting, dressing and sleeping, but it lacked facilities for
cooking, dining and worship. Additional buildings were
needed for servants, maids and other family members. They
constructed thick bamboo fencing and sheds for husking
pedals[311] and cattle—both essential to daily life. All the
construction was eventually completed.

The family started their journey from Guwahati,
intending to travel by boat through the Kolong and Sonai
rivers. However, Lambodar, one of the boatmen from
Kaliabor, warned that the water level in the Sonai was
receding and that the route via the Kolong and Sonai was
infested with mosquitoes. As a result, they altered course,
sailing upstream and docking at Laukhowa, directly across
from Tezpur. Ananda Ram was disheartened by this

---

[310] An indigenous tribe, earlier known as Lalung or Lali. This text
uses Lali.

[311] Dhenki, a kind of husking pedal operated in a see-saw manner.

change, as the remaining journey to Nagaon was roughly 26 kilometres and required travelling through a dense forest. With considerable difficulty, he managed to bring his family and their belongings safely to Nagaon.

That same year, Hudson was appointed as the new chief assistant after Butler moved to Guwahati and became its the acting deputy commissioner. Ananda Ram diligently performed his duties and spent his mornings and evenings translating for his law project. At the time, brilliant students from Bengali-medium schools were appointed as apprentices in court offices and received monthly stipends from the government. One such apprentice, Rudraram, known for his excellent handwriting, was assigned to copy Ananda Ram's translated manuscript. The final copy was sent to Nabin Babu and printed at the New Press in Calcutta.

Previously, commissioners and deputy commissioners would tour every district of Assam during winter to inspect the offices, their work and the town. This winter, Jenkins visited Nagaon. He had never visited the home of any native nor attended any weddings or ceremonies of the Phukan family in Guwahati. However, he visited Ananda Ram's home in Nagaon, which was a great honour for Ananda Ram.

Ananda Ram's guru, Parbatiya Kalidas Bhattacharya Goswami, came to Nagaon in the month of Puh.[312] Ananda Ram built a temporary house for his guru's stay at the ghat and often visited him to learn about the worship

---

[312] December–January.

rituals for his patron deity. On the Sankranti of Puh and Magh Bihu,[313] Parbatiya Gosain initiated Mahindri as his disciple and returned to Guwahati a few days later.

Hudson left Nagaon after Butler returned and resumed his duties. A Baptist missionary society[314] based in Boston, United States of America, had sent pastors to this country to propagate Christianity. Many such preachers, based in Nagaon, Sivasagar, Guwahati and other places, spread Christianity in this region. Pastors Bronson[315] and Stoddard[316] were stationed in Nagaon, which was their principal base. Dr Pack,[317] secretary of the missionary society, arrived from Boston to oversee the mission's activities. Pastors Danforth,[318] Whiting[319] and Brown[320]

---

[313] Magh Bihu is a harvest festival, celebrated in Assam on the last day of Puh.

[314] The original text mentions it as 'Baptist Missionary Christian Society'.

[315] Dr Miles Bronson of the American Baptist Mission wrote several books including an Assamese–English dictionary in 1867. In 1845 Bronson established the first Baptist church at Panbazar in Guwahati.

[316] Dr Issachar Jay Stoddard.

[317] Dr Solomon Peck, a Baptist minister and the corresponding secretary of the American Baptist Missionary Union, visited Assam in 1855.

[318] A.H. Danforth.

[319] Rev. S. W. Whiting.

[320] Dr Nathan Brown edited *Orunodoi*, the first Assamese magazine, and composed a grammar titled *Grammatical Notices of the Assamese Language* in 1848.

from Guwahati and Upper Assam held special discussions on preaching with pastors in Nagaon. Ananda Ram visited the pastors frequently, and they, in turn, visited his home. He was fascinated by their enthusiasm for religion.

Balaram arrived in Nagaon from Guwahati at the end of February. Ananda Ram was delighted to talk to him after a long time. A few young men from the Dilihiyal Bhattacharjya family, also known as the Khataniars of Bengenaati, had been residing in Guwahati. One of them, Dharmadatta—the son of Budhadatta Khataniar—had been staying with Ananda Ram for a long time. Both Ananda Ram and his wife adored this destitute man. Dharmadatta studied at the court and did daily shopping and other such chores. Ananda Ram arranged his marriage to Keteki, the daughter of Madhu Bapu from Singia Potani. Ananda Ram and his wife were delighted when the newlyweds visited their home.

Ananda Ram was entrusted the responsibility of the entire district again after Butler became the deputy commissioner of Guwahati. The Naga tribe was creating havoc back then as well. News arrived on 17 March that the Nagas had massacred people from four Karbi villages. Ananda Ram directed a police team to go there, after changing his initial decision to visit the location himself. He then reported it to the commissioner and wrote that he was ready to go there if directed. The commissioner did not order Ananda Ram to go to the spot; rather, he found an alternative way to bring the Nagas under control.

There were many small *jans*[321] in Nagaon, Chapori Mahal and other areas. Floods caused by the Brahmaputra River entered through these jans and destroyed crops. Ananda Ram was tasked with building embankments along these tributaries. He organized workers and periodically inspected the progress. Initially, the farmers were hesitant to assist, but Ananda Ram arranged a meeting with prominent villagers to persuade them. This resulted in the embankments being built at a low cost, and people gradually realized that the constructions were for their benefit. Ananda Ram travelled to different locations in the Nagaon district, including to Chapori Mahal, Jamunamukh and Kaliabor, to construct embankments on several jans, such as Gariyajan, Dimowjan and Konharjan.

Before Ananda Ram's posting in Nagaon, a junior assistant had been stationed there, but the position had been vacant since he had arrived. The government granted Ananda Ram the powers of a junior assistant in April 1854 under the provisions of the Assam Kaydabandi. He was also given the responsibilities of a sadar amin, thereby acquiring the authority to order up to one year of imprisonment. In effect, Ananda Ram served as both a deputy collector in the revenue department and a sadar amin in the civil court.

In the same month, Lieutenant Lamb[322] took charge of the Nagaon district. Ananda Ram conducted trials regularly and occasionally visited sites to initiate or

---

[321] A rivulet or a stream of a river.

[322] Lieutenant T. Lamb.

oversee embankment construction. Despite the monsoon being around the corner, the construction was not yet complete, and Lamb discouraged Ananda Ram. However, a determined Ananda Ram redoubled his efforts and managed to almost complete the project. During the monsoon, the rising waters of the Brahmaputra and the Kolong clogged many large jans as well as breached a few embankments, which could not be salvaged. Haiborgaon, which was connected to Nagaon town during Butler's tenure, lay on the opposite side of the Nagaon district headquarters at Khagarijan. A bamboo platform bridge with wooden posts connected Nagaon and Haiborgaon. The central section of the bridge was not very sturdy as it was challenging to thrust posts on river sand. During the monsoon, an abundance of reeds came floating on the Kolong, and a few got stuck to the bridge posts. On 26 June 1854, the bridge caved in the middle when a strong current pushed these reeds. The bridge was damaged further the following day as more posts gave way. Butler had built the bridge with great care and effort, and it had proven crucial in crossing over from one bank to the other.

Amritnarayan Bhup Bahadur, the raja of Bijni, passed away around the time of Ananda Ram's arrival in Nagaon. With the raja's consent, his wife Bhagyeshwari adopted Kumudnarayan, a prince from the extended family, as they had no son. The Bijni estate came under the Court of Wards, as the queen was a woman, and her son a minor. Subsequently, the estate was managed by government officials, including the collector and the commissioner. The dispute between the raja and his tenants was now to be resolved by the government. The settlement process began, and officials—a deputy collector and a sadar amin—were appointed.

Ananda Ram's salary and reward, as well as Balaram's payment, were still due. Ananda Ram submitted an application to the collector, providing an estimate and claiming some cash against the raja's property. However, the executive from the raja's administration did not consider the hard work, effort and care that Ananda Ram had put into protecting the estate, which had led to the current settlement. They dismissed Ananda Ram's claim as baseless. Agnew, the collector of Goalpara, reported to the commissioner about Ananda Ram's alleged false claim. Ananda Ram was deeply hurt; he informed the commissioner that his claims were valid and that the complaint against him was unfounded. The commissioner began an inquiry into the matter.

Meanwhile, Ananda Ram's house and gardens were neatly arranged. He had built a house with a raised platform for the bedrooms, and beautiful gardens had been set up in front of the bungalow, which served as the sitting room. He felt relieved, as the construction of the other houses was nearly complete.

Government officials made decisions on who owned tax-free land without any input from the public or landholders, and without any discussion. Ananda Ram had submitted his opinion on this matter to Mills as well.

Rowlatt,[323] the collector of Kamrup, liked and appreciated
Ananda Ram's views. Ananda Ram submitted a long essay
on tax-free land, containing extensive arguments. Rowlatt
also sought his opinion on a case regarding tax-free land,
which concerned the Parbatiya Gosains of Kamrup.

Ananda Ram's mother was from Majuli's Ahatguri
Satra. On 21 October,[324] he arranged for her visit, as she
wanted to go to her paternal home. He had a large family
to feed, for which he had to buy all the supplies. Ananda
Ram's purchased land at Balijuri in Nagaon and converted it
into an agricultural farm, which provided him with rice. He
occasionally received supplies from Guwahati too. Despite
these efforts, his salary was not enough. Ananda Ram's
was very sad, as he did not have much cash with him on
the day of his mother's departure to Majuli. She returned
from Majuli in December,[325] having had to prepone her
departure due to the impending blockage of the upper
mouth of the Kolong River at Arikatimukh.

At that time, Bengali was the official language of the
court and the medium of instruction in schools in Assam.
Reverend Bronson composed a memorandum to press for
the introduction of Assamese as the official language, with
the help of Ananda Ram. Ananda Ram was the only native
speaker who was concerned with the language issue and

---

[323] E.A. Rowlatt.

[324] In the original text, the date, 9 Ahin, was also mentioned.

[325] In the original text, the mentioned date is 29 Kati, which may be
converted as 10 December.

could advise on it. The other native gentlemen boasted of their origins in Nadia, Santipur or Kanaujpur and did not bother whether Assamese or Bengali was the official language. Though Bronson's efforts did not yield much success initially, the missionaries and Ananda Ram worked hard for the local language's development.

Ananda Ram's wife gave birth to a baby boy on 9 December 1854,[326] a Saturday. Ananda Ram rushed to bring Dr Morey to assist with the difficult labour. Fortunately, the baby was born at seven in the evening. Everyone was overjoyed, and ululation was played. Ananda Ram's first son was assigned Radhikaram as the official name and Dimbakanthi as the concealed one. The boy's birth caused Ananda Ram's wife to be ill for most of December, but she recovered by the end of the month. May God bless him with a long and prosperous life.

---

[326] In the original text, 25 Aghon 1776 Sak is also mentioned.

Chapter 6

At the beginning of 1855, Ananda Ram went on a tour of the countryside to inspect his embankment project and visited schools in the area. During his tour, he discovered that creating a small channel between the Kolong and Diphalu rivers could connect the Brahmaputra and the Kolong. This connection would allow water to flow into the Kolong year-round, even after the Arikatimukh, which is the upper mouth of the Kolong, is closed. The closure of this upper mouth during winter often leads to the Kolong drying up, causing difficulties for the local people. That is why Ananda Ram attempted to carry out the channel building. He received a warm welcome and blessings from the mahantas when he visited many ancient satras during his tour. The work of embankments on the many tributaries was completed that same year. Once, while returning from Phulaguri, the elephant on which Ananda Ram was riding accidentally slipped from the riverbank, but he survived by the grace of God.

Ananda Ram's son and daughter received their vaccinations, in keeping with the English system, in the month of Magh.[327] The girl had received another vaccine earlier. Ananda Ram regularly discussed the Assamese language with Bronson and Butler and he started compiling an Assamese dictionary, as one did not exist. Butler sent handbills to different places for subscriptions and got ninety-three customers. Ananda Ram planned to start printing the dictionary once he had 150 customers.

Lambodar Barua and his two daughters stayed with Ananda Ram. Ananda Ram arranged for Rameswari, Lambodar's elder daughter, to marry Rameswar, the nephew of Gopal Adhyapak from Puranigudam. He performed his first son's *Jatakarma*,[328] *Namkaran*[329] and *Annaprasan*[330] in the month of Ahar.[331]

Ananda Ram was a significant figure in the Assamese language movement. During that time, he wrote a book in English titled *A Few Remarks on the Assamese Language and on Vernacular Education in Assam*. He printed 100 copies of this book at the Baptist Mission Press in Sivasagar, spending Rs 40 in the process, and distributed copies among prominent people, sending a copy to the Bengal government. The book highlighted the differences between the Assamese and Bengali languages and drew attention to the independent and diverse repository of Assamese

---

[327] January–February.

[328] Hindu ritual of birth.

[329] Hindu ritual of naming an infant.

[330] A Hindu ritual of feeding a baby the first morsel of rice.

[331] May–June.

texts, including literature, plays, mathematics, medicine and history. Ananda Ram was also concerned about the destruction caused by opium in the region and intended to write an article on it. However, it did not happen, as Butler was leaving Assam. Nevertheless, he conveyed his views to the government through other means.

Around the same time, Hudson was transferred to Guwahati, Lamb was transferred to Nagaon, and there were talks of transferring Ananda Ram to Mangaldoi. Vincent,[332] the chief assistant commissioner of Darrang, tried to bring Ananda Ram to Mangaldoi, and in his letter, he noted that Ananda Ram's report on the Assamese language was similar to his own views and also matched his own report on the country's languages. 'Both are so similar that if you read either of them, it feels like both authors wrote them after discussing them with each other.' Ananda Ram took charge of the entire district after Butler went to England in November. He submitted two reports to the commissioner on serious matters regarding the resignation of land holdings and another on the *chamua* system.[333] As all tenants were directly under the government, he weighed in on the chamua system. Ananda Ram believed that there needed to be an intermediary between the government and

---

[332] Lieutenant G.F. Vincent.

[333] A class of land revenue collectors in the early decades of the East India Company rule in Assam where the revenue from small mahals were collected by *Chamuadars* and revenue was paid directly to the government.

the public for the benefit of the country. Lamb took over charge of the district in January 1856.

A half-sister of Ananda Ram's mother married Hemakantha Bezbarua. Their son, Kambukantha, came to live with Ananda Ram and, shortly after, lost his father, becoming helpless at a young age. Ananda Ram loved Kambukantha and sent him to school in Nagaon. Later, Kambukantha's mother also came to live in Nagaon. Ananda Ram sent Kambukantha to Calcutta for higher studies, covering all expenses himself. However, Kambukantha returned to Nagaon at his mother's request after a while. While in Calcutta, Kambukantha stayed with Gunabhiram. He was sent to study in Guwahati but returned after a few days, unable to adjust. Ananda Ram treated Kambukantha like his own brother, and Kambukantha respected and cared for Ananda Ram as an elder brother or father figure. He also studied very hard.

In Calcutta, Nabin Babu and Prasanna Babu were unable to continue managing the Sudder Diwani decrees and had to hand them over to others after a while. The first volume of *Notes on the Laws of Bengal* sold out quickly. The book covered a wide range of topics, including policy and regulations in India, law, rights of individuals, physical rights, rights of the king and his subjects, the British parliament and the Company office, the supreme and provincial governments and their subordinate executives and subjects. It also discussed the reciprocal rights of masters and servants, husbands and wives, parents and children, adopted sons and guardians and wards, as well as corporations, property, zamindaris and talukas under talukdars, Badshahi grants, including farmers of leased lands, leased landholders, tax-free landholders, immovable properties and rights, Hindu, Muslim and English laws of inheritance, divisible assets and division and guardianship. The book was priced at Rs 4, and Nabin Babu and Gunabhiram were responsible for sending it to customers. The book was well received by newspapers and the public, and at the request of the judges of the Sudder Diwani Court, the government purchased 250 copies for Rs 1000 and sent them to the judges. This was the first law book written in Bengali or any vernacular language, and it proved to be very helpful to the common people, written in simple language that was easily understood by all. Ananda Ram became well known through this book, which expanded the scope of the Bengali language and also contributed to the development of jurisprudence in Bengali. Nabin and Gunabhiram were responsible for circulating and marketing the book, and it was in such high demand that they had to rush to the post office every day to send it to customers.

Ananda Ram was able to save only a small amount of money from his monthly income after covering necessary expenses. He decided to give his wife a monthly allowance of Rs 25 and also converted her jewellery into *streedhan*[334] through a bond. After a while, Mahindri fell sick, and the doctor who treated her was unable to cure her. The doctor

---

[334] A Hindu woman's absolute property, free from any restrictions on her right to enjoy and transfer it.

suggested a change of air, so they decided to send her to Guwahati.

Ananda Ram's sister, Tuloshi, her husband, Raghudev, and their sons, Chandrahas, Padmahas and Tarahas, occasionally visited them from Jakhalabandha Satra. Whenever the two families met, they enjoyed their time together. Raghudev and Kambukantha accompanied Mahindri to Guwahati. She went to Guwahati on 17 June 1856,[335] with baby Padmavati and little Radhika. They stayed with Balaram in Guwahati for a month, and Mahindri recovered from her illness by enjoying the cool air of the Brahmaputra. In the last fortnight of Saon, she returned to Nagaon with Balaram. Radhika had a throat infection on this journey but recovered.

Ananda Ram often rode an elephant or a horse to enjoy the countryside around Nagaon. Dr Mouat, the inspector general of the jail, came to Nagaon for a visit and was delighted to meet Ananda Ram after a long time. Mahindri delivered a boy, Annadaram, at nine in the morning on Saturday, 27 December 1856.[336] She did not undergo a very painful labour this time. Ananda Ram and his friends were overjoyed at the arrival of this son. May God grant him a long and blessed life!

Ananda Ram's grandmother, who lived with Balaram, visited Nagaon for a few days. She was delighted to meet Ananda Ram and his children. Sadly, she passed away soon

---

[335] In the original, the date 5 Ahar 1778 Sak was also mentioned.,
[336] In the original, the date 14 Puh, 1778 Sak was also mentioned.

after returning to Guwahati. Ananda Ram was deeply saddened by the news and managed the arrangements for her shraddha from Nagaon. Lamb left Nagaon when Butler returned from his leave. Purnananda Baruah from the Bezbarua family visited Ananda Ram in Nagaon in early January. Ananda Ram was thrilled to hear the news from Upper Assam.

Gunabhiram resided with Nabin Babu in Calcutta and was admitted to Kolutola Branch School. After qualifying for the junior scholarship examination, Gunabhiram joined Presidency College. He studied there for two years but failed to pass the second-year annual examination. Although he wanted to study medicine at medical college, Ananda Ram advised against it, and so he joined the law course at that college. In the beginning, Gunabhiram's monthly expenses were no more than Rs 8, which was adjusted with the printing cost of Ananda Ram's book. However, the fee for the law course was Rs 5 per month. Nabin Babu and Gunabhiram would occasionally courier books and other items purchased by Ananda Ram from Calcutta. After becoming acquainted with Calcutta, Gunabhiram managed everything there. Ananda Ram informed the Revenue Board and the government about his claims from the Bijni raja after not receiving a favourable decision from the collector and the commissioner. Thereafter, Ananda Ram appointed Gunabhiram as his representative, and as a result, the board returned the papers to the commissioner for revision. Ananda Ram was pleased with Gunabhiram's progress in education.

Mahindri's brother, Durgachandra, and sister, Brajasundari, lived at their home in Jorhat. Durgachandra was initiated into the sacred thread by Balaram Deka Phukan. Brajasundari had also reached a marriageable age. Though they lived in Jorhat, Ananda Ram and Mahindri were still their guardians. They wished for Durgachandra and Brajasundari to live with them. They hoped to marry off Brajasundari to Gunabhiram and also wanted to settle Durgachandra in either Guwahati or Nagaon once he completed his studies and married. Ananda Ram wrote to Balaram Deka Phukan, proposing Brajasundari's marriage to Gunabhiram and the sending of Durgachandra. Deka Phukan gave his consent to these proposals.

Ananda Ram also wrote to Nabin and Gunabhiram regarding the marriage proposal for Brajasundari. Nabin agreed, but Gunabhiram refused. He argued that marriage would disrupt his education and make it difficult for him to return to Calcutta afterward. His other objection was that he did not consider himself suitable for marriage. He explained that he had not initiated himself to a guru, as he regarded the practice as baseless. His religious beliefs were also unconventional as he was inclined towards the Brahmo Samaj. He rejected the proposal on these grounds. Extensive correspondence followed between Gunabhiram and Ananda Ram. Gunabhiram also stated that he was not rich enough to live independently. Mahindri was very upset by this development. She noted that Gunabhiram's apprehension about property was valid but assured him that it did not matter. They would wholeheartedly support him, as he was part of their family. Nevertheless, Gunabhiram declined the proposal. A very upset Ananda Ram and Mahindri wrote a letter about it to Deka Phukan. They eventually arranged for Brajasundari's marriage elsewhere, as it was no longer possible to leave her unmarried.

After much consideration, Gunabhiram wrote to Ananda Ram in February, stating that he would agree to the marriage on the condition that he could only come during the month of Kati.[337] Phukan agreed and conveyed the message to Brajasundari's family, who were all delighted.

Ananda Ram raised the idea of setting up a charity hospital with Butler, and Butler agreed. However, the project did not materialize, as no native wanted to donate due to their aversion to foreign medicine and treatment.

After Colonel Vetch left, Butler replaced him as the deputy commissioner of Kamrup. Morton took charge of Nagaon. News of the sepoy mutiny came from the Western Province, and daily reports of the rogue sepoys' violence against the British began to arrive from various places. Shortly after Mills's visit to Assam, Kandarpeswar Singha, the grandson of King Purandar Singha of Jorhat,

---

[337] October–November.

deputed Maniram Dewan[338] to negotiate for his kingship. When Kandarpeswar, with Maniram's suggestion and the support of the military posted in Upper Assam, was about to launch a mutiny, he was sent to Calcutta. The trial began. The province, particularly Upper Assam, was in turmoil. Morton in Nagaon became very concerned. Bridges over the Misa and Diju rivers were destroyed on Morton's orders, as he feared the sepoys would use these bridges to reach Nagaon from the upper region. He distrusted all natives. Almost all missionaries stationed in Nagaon returned to America. Ananda Ram was deeply saddened and worried by the news of violence from different parts of the country. He wrote to assure the British officers that the Assamese people would not rebel against them, but no one took note of his concerns.

In the August–September[339] months of 1857,[340] Balaram Phukan visited Nagaon for a few days. Ananda Ram sent Joymati, a Brahmin widow who lived with them, to Jorhat to fetch Durgachandra and Brajasundari. He also asked Gunabhiram to return soon, assuring him of his early return after marriage. Gunabhiram returned home

---

[338] Maniram Barbhandar Barua (1806–57), better known as Maniram Dewan, the prime minister to the last Ahom king and later an official of the Assam Company, and himself a tea entrepreneur, was hanged for his involvement in the Sepoy Mutiny.

[339] Saon.

[340] 1779 Sak.

from Calcutta by boat at the end of the month of Ahin.[341]
He came to Nagaon after staying a few days in Guwahati.
Gunabhiram and Brajasundari's wedding ceremony
was celebrated on 2 December 1857.[342] Durgachandra
performed the *kanyaadaan*[343] ritual in the wedding. Ananda
Ram and Mahindri were overjoyed by the marriage. The
event brought so much joy to the family that even little
Padma, sitting in a palanquin and carrying a tiny pitcher,
joined the wedding procession to fetch water from the
river to bathe the bride and groom. Gunabhiram's aunt and
sister-in-law came from Guwahati to attend the wedding.
The wedding made Gunabhiram's sister, the wife of the
Deka Gosain of Diphalu Satra, very happy. The main reason
behind Ananda Ram and Mahindri's happiness was that
both the groom and bride were under their care, and that
the two families, who were already close, would now grow
even closer and bond more deeply through this marriage.

Gunabhiram appeared for the first-year law examination,
with two more to go: the first next month and the final one
in March. He decided to go to Calcutta in January 1858
to appear for the March examination. Durgachandra and
Kambukantha also wanted to go with Gunabhiram to study
in Guwahati. Despite their family's objections, they began

---

[341] September–October.

[342] In the original text, 18 Aghon is also mentioned.

[343] Ritualistic giving away of a bride to a groom in a Hindu marriage.

their journey on 21 January.[344] That day, Ananda Ram and Mahindri were quite sad, and Ananda Ram even cried. After reaching Guwahati, Gunabhiram received a letter from them forbidding him from going to Calcutta. More than Ananda Ram, Mahindri was more forthright in her disapproval. Ananda Ram assured Gunabhiram that they would study law together if he agreed to return. He also urged Gunabhiram to consult Jenkins. After considering all this, Gunabhiram decided not to go and returned to Nagaon in Fagun[345] with Kambukantha. Durgachandra, who had stayed in Guwahati with Balaram, took admission in a school.

Ananda Ram received a raise of Rs 100 in addition to his existing salary of Rs 250 after completing five years of service on 14 October 1858. This was the norm, and the order was issued on 4 December of the same year. In January 1858, he visited Kaliabor and completed his work in a mouza[346] there. He then went to Borghop, where he noticed that the distance between the Kolong and Brahmaputra was only thirty feet.[347] Water from the Brahmaputra could be channelled into the Kolong by digging this land. He was

---

[344] In the original text, the mentioned date is 7 Magh, which may be converted as 21 January.

[345] February–March.

[346] A revenue division of a district under a revenue collector called mouzadar.

[347] Twenty hands or *haath* (hand) in the original text. One standard hand is equal to one cubit in length, which is equal to 1.5 feet.

thrilled to see the Brahmaputra again after 15 July 1853, when he entered Kolong from the river while sailing to Nagaon. Ananda Ram also visited Arikatimukh, the upper mouth of the Kolong, where a sandbar developed in the winter. After performing other official duties, he returned to Nagaon.

During this period, a European named Lyall[348] attempted to establish a tea garden in Nagaon. In Nagaon, a Roman Catholic doctor named Pingault[349] built a church and started a tea garden at Samaguri in Bheleuguri mouza. After his death, Barry from Sirajganj purchased the tea estate, the doctor's bungalow and other properties. Barry later established another tea garden at Madartoli.[350] Dharmadatta was appointed as the manager of the Chamaguri tea garden, and Barry entrusted Ananda Ram with the full responsibility of the garden. Shortly after, Herriott[351] became Barry's partner. With Ananda Ram's help, Dharmadatta established a weekly haat[352] that still exists today. Morton, the chief assistant of Nagaon, fell ill and went to Guwahati before returning to England. Ananda Ram was given full charge of the district again.

The Kolong had a great bend, known as Morikolong Bend, to the west of the jail in Nagaon. As the bend could

---

[348] Robert Lyall.

[349] Dr F. Pingault.

[350] Madartollah tea estate having 18911 acres of grant.

[351] James Herriot.

[352] A local market.

be removed by cutting through thirty feet of land, Ananda Ram tried to get the prisoners to cut this distance. Their efforts shortened the water flow by around two miles. This point is still known as Khanajan,[353] or Khanajanmukh. The channel that was left aside is known as the Pota[354] Kolong. Ananda Ram took the initiative to cut several other bends of the river near Mowamari and other places. He was once supposed to be transferred to Mangaldoi, but it did not happen. On another occasion, there were rumours that Beckett would be transferred to Nagaon.

The kings of Koch Bihar, a tributary state, are considered descendants of Lord Shiva. The post of dewan of the state became vacant after the death of Dewan Kalichandra Lahiri. Ananda Ram wrote to the commissioner, hoping to be appointed to that post, but someone else was appointed even before he could send the letter.

A severe famine occurred in Nagaon that year, causing rice prices to skyrocket to four annas[355] per seer.[356] This was an unprecedented event in the region. People who had paddy in their granaries hoarded their stocks, hoping to make more profit as the prices increased. However, rice supplies from the west stopped, and the autumn rice[357]

---

[353] The stream that has been dug.

[354] Filled up.

[355] One-fourth of a rupee.

[356] A measurement of weight used before metrication. One seer is equivalent to 870.89 grams in Assam and Bengal.

[357] Ahu rice.

harvesting season was still a few months away. Adding
to the misery, the entire *keyanpatty*,[358] the business centre
of Nagaon, was destroyed by a fire in March. People were
suffering greatly.

To address the dire situation, Ananda Ram ordered
hoarders to sell their paddy for cash. Those who refused
would have their granaries broken into, and their paddy
would be distributed to victims, on the condition that they
pay with cash or paddy after the next harvest. Although
this system would be unreasonable in normal times, it
was appropriate during the famine and saved many lives.
After Ananda Ram wrote to him, the commissioner also
approved of this measure. Ananda Ram also submitted a
proposal for selling rice procured from government stock.
The commissioner agreed to this proposal and wrote to the
government about it. However, the government later passed
a declaration stating that traders could procure rice instead,
as the government did not want to be involved in the rice
business. The conditions improved after the autumn rice
harvest, with many traders bringing in rice from other areas.
This famine was not specific to Nagaon; it was widespread
during that time. Without rice, their primary staple food,
many turned to yams and leafy greens for survival. This
famine is still remembered today as the Great Famine and
also as the year when granaries were broken into. During
this period, a comet appeared in the sky for a few days.[359]

---

[358] An alley of Marwari businessmen.

[359] Most probably it was the comet Donati, which was visible in
India for several months in 1858, first observed on 2 June 1858.

After Dr Pingault passed away, there were no European physicians available in Nagaon. A new doctor, named Dr Lee,[360] arrived during the monsoon season, but unfortunately, he died soon after. Mahindri fell ill again, and as her condition did not improve, she was taken upstream on the Kolong to Biswanath for a change of air. She returned shortly after. In 1858, a regulation was introduced that made stamping on documents compulsory in the province of Assam. Ananda Ram appointed Shambhuram's son, Prithuram Barua, as the stamp vendor. Previously, the road between Morikolong and Dabaka was not in good condition. However, a new road was built between Morikolong and Pathari under the supervision of Ananda Ram, who ensured that the road was constructed properly.

Towards the end of August, Lt Scones[361] became the chief assistant in Nagaon. Court petitions written by laypeople had harmed the plaintiffs. To remedy this, Ananda Ram appointed two petition writers, Kirtikanta Barua and Kamalakanta Bhuyan, after testing them in consultation with Scones. Babu Kishorichand Mitra, a junior magistrate in Calcutta, retired from his post. Ananda Ram wanted to apply for that position, but since he would have had to leave Assam, he abandoned his plan. Ananda Ram was a devoted patriot. In a trial conducted in Upper

---

[360] Dr A.C. Lee.

[361] Lieutenant Herbert Sconce.

Assam, Maniram Dewan and Piyali[362] were sentenced to death, while Dutiram Chirastadar and several others received jail terms. The mutiny inquiry team sent their spy to Nagaon to secretly investigate Ananda Ram's loyalty, but they did not find anything incriminating. Meanwhile, a daily newspaper from Calcutta called *Bengal Harkara*[363] published an anonymous letter that hinted at Ananda Ram's involvement in the mutiny and his sympathy for the mutineers. The letter also claimed that Ananda Ram once went to Laokhowa to meet Prince Kandarpeswar Singha while he was being taken to Calcutta.[364] Ananda Ram was saddened and astonished after reading the letter. He wrote letters to the commissioner, deputy commissioners and all chief assistants of the districts, asking for their opinions on the issue. Everyone reiterated that he was innocent and maintained that they had not heard anything against him. As the allegations against Ananda Ram could not be proved, the collector of Goalpara withdrew his complaint on the order of the commissioner in the Bijni case and acknowledged his mistake in a letter.

In 1858, Her Highness the Queen took control of India from the East India Company. On 19 November of the same year, a proclamation was read out, and a large

---

[362] Piyali Barua was hanged along with Maniram for his role in Sepoy Mutiny in Assam.

[363] *The Bengal Hurkaru and Chronicle* was an English newspaper published from Calcutta.

[364] 'West' in the original text.

crowd gathered in front of the collectorate. Ananda Ram translated the proclamation into Assamese and then read out the English version. Ratneswar, the superintendent of the collectorate, read out the Bengali version; while Jagabandhu, the superintendent of the civil court, read out the Urdu version; and Habiram, the superintendent of the criminal court, read out the Assamese version. The soldiers offered a gun salute and earthen lamps were lit at night to create a pattern that read: 'Long Live the Queen'. Later that night, the Mahantas of Narowa and Solguri performed the traditional *bhaona*,[365] which attracted a lot of people to the town. However, a dispute arose over who would get more prominence among the Mahantas, which Ananda Ram resolved. Overall, the celebration was very well organized.

Lambodar Deka Barua's second daughter was staying with Ananda Ram at this time. Ananda Ram arranged her marriage with Jaydev Mahanta, who belonged to the Laiatiya Satra. During the wedding ceremony, Gunabhiram gave away the bride[366] as her father was unwell at that time.

In 1858, Ananda Ram purchased the Company's promissory note worth Rs 5000 at an annual interest rate of 5 per cent through Mr Becher of Guwahati. This was Ananda Ram's first savings endeavour.

---

[365] A traditional theatrical performance that originated in fifteenth-century Assam.

[366] Sampradan.

Chapter 7

Thus, 1858 ended and 1859 began. Ananda Ram was twenty-nine years, three months and ten days old on the first of January that year. Captain Comber[367] took charge of the Nagaon district from Ananda Ram at the beginning of the month. Prior to that, a government circular notified that Ananda Ram would serve as the chief assistant commissioner with full power in the absence of the designated officer. Ananda Ram was fulfilling his duties accordingly.

Mahindri delivered a baby girl on 21 January.[368] The girl, not of a very fair complexion, was named Chandra, or Chandraprabha. Mahindri's labour was not very painful this time.

Commissioner Jenkins toured Upper Assam that winter. His itinerary did not include Nagaon due to some inconvenience. Ananda Ram wanted to travel to Tezpur to meet him and hoped to make the visit during his Kaliabor

---

[367] A.K. Comber.

[368] In the original text, 9 Magh 1780 Sak is also mentioned.

tour, to which Comber agreed. Ananda Ram began his journey on 1 February. He reached Kamakhya at Kaliabor after resolving land disputes on the way. On 7 February, he arrived in Tezpur and met Jenkins. He was delighted to meet his old friend Parashuram Baruah, a clerk at the commissioner's office, who was accompanying Jenkins on his tour.

In Calcutta, there are several life insurance companies. The amount of insured money the family receives upon the death of the insured member is determined by the amount of the monthly instalment. Ananda Ram wanted to take out a life insurance policy for Rs 10,000. One has to undergo a health check-up by a gazetted physician before taking out a life insurance policy. The company insures a person only after the doctor gives a satisfactory health report. Ananda Ram applied to the company for a life insurance policy. The company asked for a doctor's certificate. As Nagaon did not have any European gazetted doctors at the time, he went to Tezpur for a check-up. He sent the doctor's report to the company after his check-up was done by Dr Lynch[369] in Tezpur.

He returned to Kaliabor after meeting the gentlemen in Tezpur. He reached Nagaon on 12 February after performing his duties there. Shortly thereafter, Parashuram arrived in Nagaon with Jenkins's permission. Balaram Phukan, too, arrived from Guwahati. Durgachandra had also returned a few days earlier. Ananda Ram was

---

[369] Dr S.J. Lynch was appointed at Tezpur in 1858.

delighted to see them all. They spent the next few days
together. Their joy knew no bounds. The mealtimes in the
mornings and evenings were greatly enjoyable. On some
days, they kept the fun going until midnight, though their
idea of 'fun' was not vulgar or meaningless. One evening,
Ananda Ram visited the jail, accompanied by Balaram,
Parashuram and Gunabhiram. There, they checked their
weight on a weighing machine that was meant for the
prisoners. Ananda Ram weighed 57 kilogrammes,[370]
Balaram 83 kilogrammes,[371] Parashuram almost 50
kilogrammes,[372] Gunabhiram 45 kilogrammes[373] and
Golap Singh, the jailor, 80 kilogrammes.[374]

Meanwhile, Radhika's churakaran rite was performed
in March.[375] While performing the Adhibas[376] ritual,
Ananda Ram sat with Radhika. Balaram remarked that
they were 'God's playthings'. Balaram and the others left
for Guwahati after this ceremony. Kambukantha married
Hemai Kataki's daughter Luduri, aka Lakkhmi, after a
short while. Ananda Ram and Mahindri were delighted to

---

[370] 1 mound 18 seer.

[371] 2 mound 4 seer.

[372] 1 ¼ mound ½ seer.

[373] 1 mound 5 seer.

[374] 2 mounds.

[375] In the original text, the mentioned date is 24 Fagun, which may
be converted as 13 March.

[376] A preliminary ceremony performed on the day previous to a
solemn rite.

fix the marriage of the boy under their mentoring. Annada's churakaran was performed on May.[377]

Meanwhile, the Act 8 of 1859[378] was implemented. Ananda Ram wanted to publish a book with a translation of the act along with rules and examples and began the translation. His friend and mentor Bland sahab came to Nagaon at the end of May. Ananda Ram was delighted to meet and talk to him.

Thus, ended the month of May. Ananda Ram's youngest daughter suffered from dysentery at the beginning of June. She was so critical that Ananda Ram had to return early from the court. Thankfully, she recovered after treatment. Mahindri too recovered after suffering from dysentery.

Ananda Ram deliberated extensively on ancient traditions and rituals. His opinion on the Hindu rituals of fasting on Ekadashi and skipping dinner on Amavashya[379] was that indigestion and bodily fluids[380] are relieved by observing fasts. The moon has an intimate relation with the earth. That is why tides in seas and adjacent rivers rise and fall according to lunar dates. Likewise, bodily fluids get drawn into this cycle. Tides increase during the period from

---

[377] In the original text, the date is 27 Bohag, which may be converted as 13 May.

[378] The Code of Civil Procedure Act 8 of 1859 codified the procedures of civil courts, excluding those established by the Royal Charter.

[379] The new moon night.

[380] Rasa.

Ekadashi to the full moon and decreased from Ekadashi to the new moon. Therefore, it had been decided to fast on Ekadashi, and night fasting was prescribed for new-moon nights. After considering all this, Ananda Ram started observing the Ekadashi *vrat* and having a small amount of rice at night for a short while.

On Saturday, 11 June,[381] Ananda Ram left for his office after drinking some water, as it was an Ekadashi. He returned from the court at four in the afternoon with a headache, body ache and fever that had begun while he was in his office. Unfortunately, there were no European doctors available in Nagaon at the time, so a native doctor named Keramat Ali[382] visited Ananda Ram and prescribed application of European vinegar on his head and a dose of James Powder.[383] At nine at night, Ananda Ram, following the doctor's advice, drank five-six spoons of tea. However, he could not sleep well that night and complained of a burning sensation in his body, particularly in his hands and feet.

---

[381] In the original text, 28 Jyeshtha 1781 Sak is also mentioned.

[382] Most probably, he was the same Keramat Ali, who studied in Calcutta Medical College in the early 1850s. See p. 82.

[383] Dr James Fever Powder, a popular patent medicine created by English physician Dr Robert James. His 'Fever Powder' claimed to be able to cure a wide array of ailments, including gout, scurvy, general fevers and even distemper, a viral disease found in dogs and cattle.

The next morning, at 5 a.m., on the doctor's advice, Ananda Ram took a purgative of senna[384] and salt. He visited the lavatory about a dozen times that day and became so weak that his wife had to assist him. At 11 a.m., he had a few spoons of sago and arrowroot with sugar candy balls[385] one or two raisins. He suffered from diarrhoea throughout the day and complained of an extreme burning sensation and headache. His fever seemed to subside a little. In the evening, he met a few native clerks and a Marwari businessman in the living room at the bungalow before returning to his room, where he had sago and tea, followed by the medicine given by the doctor. Unfortunately, he could not sleep well that night, and the next morning, his fever returned.

The doctor came again and examined Ananda Ram. He prescribed a white syrup, which Ananda Ram drank. He was moved from his bedroom on a raised platform to the bungalow, which was made of concrete and better equipped for the circumstances. His fever suddenly spiked very high. The doctor gave him the same medicine again, and Mahindri trimmed Ananda Ram's neck-length hair to a very short length on the doctor's advice. Ananda Ram profusely perspired after being covered under layers of clothes. The doctor wished to administer quinine, but Ananda Ram and Mahindri wondered whether it was truly

---

[384] *Sonamukhi (Cassia angustifolia)* in Assamese. A medicinal plant whose pods and leaves are used as a laxative.

[385] Ola, ball or laddu made of *mishri*, or sugar candy.

necessary. The doctor confirmed it was, and so Ananda Ram took quinine every hour. The doctor also gave him a laxative, which caused him to go to the lavatory several times, weakening him further.

At around 4 p.m., Ananda Ram said he was having difficulty hearing soft speech. He kept lemon slices and raisin water in his mouth occasionally, as he felt very thirsty. He started vomiting, which made it difficult for him to take the medicines. Since he was unable to eat sago and arrowroot, the doctor advised him to have sour rice gruel[386] with green gram dal. It was a struggle for him to eat the meal, but he managed. He had trouble sleeping that night and had to make frequent trips to the bathroom. He passed yellow or reddish-green stools and became so weak that he had to use a chair as a toilet. His wife had to clean it afterwards. The doctor examined the stool and diagnosed it as containing bile.

The next day, the doctor announced that Ananda Ram's fever had subsided. However, some native clerks disagreed with the doctor's assessment and suggested using native medicine instead of European treatment. But Ananda Ram refused to take native medicine. The doctor gave him laxatives when he vomited, yet the vomiting continued. At 3 p.m., the doctor applied a mustard poultice to Ananda Ram's abdomen, which was removed an hour later. Ananda Ram became almost unconscious, and the doctor gave

---

[386] *Kanzi.*

him another laxative. He could not sleep that night as he frequently went to the toilet.

The following morning, the doctor declared that Ananda Ram had recovered, and Ananda Ram agreed, feeling much better. The doctor gave him another laxative, leading to several more bowel movements. Ananda Ram, who usually shaved every other day, had to skip shaving due to his illness. He shaved at noon and then read a newspaper called *The Phoenix* and a book titled *Graham's Domestic Medicine* at 2 p.m. He asked Gunabhiram to read the book aloud, but Gunabhiram, suffering from a severe headache, was unable to do so. Kambukantha read a few pages to Ananda Ram.

At 2.30 in the afternoon, the fever returned, and Ananda Ram began sweating heavily. The doctor gave him another laxative. Kalicharan Biswas, a Bengali officer in the revenue department, visited him. Ananda Ram said a few lines in Bengali to him. Kalicharan left after the lights were turned on, and Ananda Ram did not speak Assamese again after that. He only spoke in Sanskrit and Bengali, including to his mother and wife.

By nine o'clock at night, Ananda Ram's condition became critical. The doctor administered medicine more frequently, and Ananda Ram was fed sago and arrowroot every time he received his medicine. He slipped into delirium and once told the doctor, 'Please make me well, and you will see what I will do to you.' After regaining his senses, Ananda Ram told Gunabhiram in English, 'Most probably, I went to hell, and now I know that I have returned from there. If the native doctor succeeds in my treatment, it will be a miracle. People will be astonished at how this doctor has cured me.' He then asked Gunabhiram in Bengali to take care of his wife and children, get the children educated and never to take native medicines. He spoke these sentences in literary Bengali.

In English, he said, 'I have done my best for the country and never harmed anyone. People may presume me to be a Christian, but I am not a Christian; I believe in God.' Throughout his illness, he occasionally invoked the name of God in a solemn voice.

While the doctor was trying to feed him medicine, Ananda Ram shouted at him in Hindustani, 'I am an assistant, whereas you are a native doctor, and you are trying to kill the magistrate. Call the police. Where has Gopal Singh, the police officer, gone?' He repeatedly asked Gunabhiram to note down everything he said, but Gunabhiram did not write anything down, thinking that Ananda Ram was delirious.

Some more medicines were required, but the doctor did not have them. So, he sent the pharmacist, Hodok, and Gunabhiram to the jail to fetch the medicine. Ananda Ram requested Gunabhiram to perform this last duty for him, having fulfilled his own duty to Gunabhiram. Mahindri asked him, 'What have you done to us?' and, placing her hand on his chest, Ananda Ram cried out, 'What can I do?' Before this, he had kept them updated about his health in Bengali and urged them not to be sad. Sometimes, he reported being unconscious. His restlessness increased so much that Ananda Ram asked the doctor to administer a syringe.[387]

The doctor administered a blister known as *liquor lyttae*[388] on Ananda Ram's neck, but it had no effect. Leeches were then applied, but they drained a lot of blood without any improvement. Ananda Ram had an urge to urinate but was unable to do so. The doctor then administered a drug called morphia. Previously, the doctor had informed the family about the uses and benefits of all drugs and consulted with them before administering any treatment. However, he did not do so before giving Ananda Ram morphia.

Ananda Ram lost consciousness after taking this medicine and was unable to speak. This was the last medicine given to him, and thereafter, he was fed only soda water. The doctor informed the family that Ananda Ram had lost consciousness due to the sedative. He was talking about morphia in all probability. The drug has this effect on humans. Ananda Ram's breathing became noisy, and the doctor asked Gunabhiram to shout near Ananda Ram's ear. The doctor then inserted hot water into Ananda Ram's ears using a syringe, but it proved ineffective.

The night passed, and morning came. The last signs of death, such as discoloured nails and a pinched nose, were visible on his body, but it still felt warm. Several tablets were

---

[387] In the original text, *piskari*.

[388] Doctors treating cholera in the 1800s described liquor lyttae and the blister as two separate consecutive acts.

administered, including Laxmivilash,[389] Nilakantha,[390] Betal[391] and Chakresar.[392] His breathing grew heavier just before nine in the morning, and he was taken outside. Though laden with grief, his wife performed the final rituals for a dying person, offering handfuls of sesame, a little gold[393] and a Boitoroni cow.[394] Ananda Ram passed away shortly thereafter, at 9 a.m. on 16 June 1859, a Thursday.[395] He was twenty-nine years, nine months and twenty-nine days old on that day.

The house was filled with cries of grief as people gathered from Nagaon and other places seven or eight kilometres away. The crowd resembled a Bijoya Dashami[396] celebration, but here, everyone was lamenting. But what could be done before God's will? Ananda Ram's body, placed on a bedstead with a mosquito net, was taken to a shaded spot under a banyan tree near the river, to the south-west of his house and the north-west of the jail, accompanied by

---

[389] A kind of Ayurvedic medicine.

[390] A kind of Ayurvedic medicine.

[391] A kind of Ayurvedic medicine.

[392] A kind of Ayurvedic medicine.

[393] *Til Kanchan*.

[394] In Hindu tradition, a cow is believed to guide one to cross the Boitoroni River near hell after death.

[395] In the original text, the first day of the dark fortnight of 3 Ahar 1781 Sak as well as the Bengali year 1266 are also mentioned.

[396] The day of the immersion of Goddess Durga when a large crowd assemble to watch the spectacle.

the sound of a beating drum.[397] Gunabhiram made Ananda Ram's eldest son, Radhikaram, who was in his lap, perform the Mukhagni[398] ritual and offer the pinda. The ritual was completed around three in the afternoon. Ananda Ram's wife, mother, stepmother, associates, dependants, servants, friends, relatives and the townspeople wailed for him. A memorial with a raised earth bed was constructed at the spot where Ananda Ram had been cremated. People from different places visited the site for many days to express their sorrow, respect and gratitude towards him.

The news of Ananda Ram's death spread quickly. Letters were sent to his friends to inform them of the sad news. His friends, Assamese, Bengali and English, expressed their shock at his passing. Some wrote letters of condolence to Gunabhiram and Radhikaram, while others shared the news with their own acquaintances. The *Orunodoi* newspaper in Assam, along with other newspapers in Calcutta and beyond, published his obituary in their editorials or letters to the editor sections.

Some believed that his death was the result of the doctor's treatment, while others blamed the excessive use of laxatives, which had weakened him and worsened his illness. A few even claimed that his death was the will of God, sharing stories of dreams in which a white elephant came to take Ananda Ram to heaven. These rumours and

---

[397] Dhol-Khol, as in the original text, are two types of drums.

[398] The ritual of putting fire on the face of the corpse before lighting the funeral pile.

speculations spread widely. Ultimately, it was concluded that the inaccurate treatment and repeated use of laxatives had weakened him to the point of no recovery. In the end, everyone agreed that it was God's will.

After receiving the heart-rending news, Balaram came from Guwahati. Gunabhiram held Radhikaram's hands and offered the Dasa Pindas.[399] Harakanta Bhattacharjya, son of Ananda Ram's teacher Kalidatta Adhyapak, and Ram Misra Nazir officiated as priests. On the eleventh day after his death, and the second day after the completion of the impurity period,[400] Mahindri performed the first shraddha[401] and offered various articles to the deceased.[402] Offerings of bulls and rice were also made that day, and honorariums were presented to the Brahmins who had come from different places. A shraddha for the soul's well-being was performed the following day.[403] The death ritual was concluded by organizing a feast for the relatives[404] on the thirteenth day. The offerings and donations were properly divided among gurus, priests and relatives. Unfortunately, some friends and relatives, who had forgotten all the help

---

[399] The Hindu ritual of offering pindas every day for ten days after one's death.

[400] *Osous*, the ceremonial impurity or defilement caused by the birth of a child or the death of a close relative in Hindu tradition.

[401] *Adya* shraddha.

[402] *Barotsarga*.

[403] Sapindikaran shraddha.

[404] *Giyati-bhojan*.

they had received from Ananda Ram during his lifetime, returned the offerings, deeming them inappropriate.

At the time of Ananda Ram's passing, he was living with a large family. This included his fifty-year-old mother, his forty-six-year-old stepmother and his twenty-six-year-old wife. His daughter Padmavati was seven years, five months and seven days old; Radhika was five years, seven months and seven days old; Annada was two years, five months and two days old; and Chandraprabha was four months and twenty-six days old. One of Ananda Ram's grandmothers[405] lived with Balaram in Guwahati. Ananda Ram considered Gunabhiram and his wife Brajasundari as part of his family, and they too lived with him. The household also included Dharmadatta, his wife Keteki, Durgachandra, Kambukantha, Kirtikanta, Lambodar, Powalchandra, Nandaram and Prithuram Barua. Botu Tamuly from Nagsankar, Jogai Thakur's son Tuloshiram, Harakanta Bapu and Khargeswar also stayed with them. Gangaram's widow Bidya, Lambodar's daughter Sandhya and Joymoti Brahmani were also part of the family. Balo, Ananda Ram's valet, stayed there with his wife and children. Madhu, Haliram's peon, lived there with his sons, Dayaram and Maniram, and their families. Raghudev Goswami and his family often stayed with them as well. Even when they lived separately, they were still regarded as part of the family. The household had several maids, including Juti, Sonaphuli and Rupohi. In addition, there was one

---

[405] Haliram Dhekiyal Phukan's stepmother.

coachman and a Kachari[406] servant with their families. Two widows had taken shelter in the Phookan house. Ananda Ram was the only breadwinner and decision-maker of the family. Unfortunately, Ananda Ram's death left them all helpless and torn apart. What is God's will? His will remains supreme.

---

[406] The term Kacharis has been used historically to denote a number of communities across the Brahmaputra valley, and adjoining hilly areas, including Bodo, Rabha and Dimasa.

Chapter 8

Ananda Ram Dhekial Phookan was fair skinned but not as white as Europeans. He was 5 feet 6 inches[407] tall, with a broad forehead, a pointed, long nose and a longish neck. He had a pair of red lips, with the lower one slightly bigger than the upper. He had a broad chest and a regular, narrow waist. His fingers and nails were average. He was neither thin nor fat and had a long face that suited his body type. He had chest hair and wide-set white teeth and weighed 54 kilogrammes in February 1859. He grew his moustache, which had not yet fully curled. He shaved every alternate day. He had a long line on his foot,[408] and the fate line on his hand[409] was complete. Ananda Ram kept neck-length hair with curly ends, and could ride a horse, though he did not know how to climb a tree, wrestle, swim or shoot.

---

[407] In the original text, three and a half hands.

[408] Hindu astrology suggests that a long fate line on the foot indicates a happy and prosperous life.

[409] Hindu astrology suggests that a complete and deep fate line is an indicator of a long and prosperous life.

Once, Balaram gave him a small pistol to fire, but he struggled to use it, and Balaram teased him for it. Ananda Ram had a habit of measuring his rice, which Balaram linked to Ananda Ram's pistol mishap. Ananda Ram had good health and did not suffer from any serious ailments. The fever that caused his death was unlike any he had ever experienced. He had suffered from fever and measles sixteen years earlier while in Calcutta but did not have any chronic illnesses. Occasionally, he had a cold or mild fevers. Once, he took a laxative while suffering from a cold, which caused him trouble. After that, he vowed never to take laxatives during the cold. He visited the lavatory twice daily after his meal and was very particular about it. He would have a decoction of haritaki[410] for mild constipation and if that did not work, he would take a laxative. He panicked whenever he suffered a bout of mild diarrhoea or cold and would consult a physician for treatment. He believed in traditional Indian medicine but could not rely on quacks. After Kambukantha stayed with him, he began to adopt a few traditional medicines and practices. He had mild pain in his knee towards the end of his life. He always wore a flannel half-sleeved vest or kurta. Just before his death, Ananda Ram could not tolerate the pain from an infection on his toenail, which caused him significant stress.

---

[410] Chebulic Myrobalan.

Someone compared the infection to a monkey's wound,[411] which made everybody laugh.

He was very particular about his diet, often having a small bowl of rice with a bowl of vegetables to avoid indigestion. A non-vegetarian, he regularly included meat in one of his daily meals, and he had pigeon curry or soup every day. He did not have a particular liking or dislike for any food, relishing all tastes—bitter, sweet, hot, sour, alkaline and astringent.[412]

He always woke up just before sunrise, and sometimes even earlier, to study and take a morning walk. Occasionally, he would read the newspaper while walking. If he could not walk due to rain or illness, he would stroll on the veranda for the same amount of time. After returning from his walk, he would study until eight and then take a warm shower. Following his shower and morning rituals, he would have breakfast at ten before heading to the collectorate. After returning from the office, he would rest and have some snacks before going out for an evening stroll or riding in a palanquin or on horseback. He would then study until eight, perform his evening rituals, have dinner and rest before going to bed around ten. He was very punctual in his sleeping, dining and strolling habits, rarely deviating from his routine. Occasionally, just before his shower after study time and in the evening before going inside, he would play

---

[411] It is an Assamese idiom, which states that a small issue can escalate if one continues to sulk.

[412] The taste of a haritaki.

like a child, pushing his childhood friends Kalikrisha and
Kirtikanta in jest and having fun.

When he first began attending court, he would wear a
pajama,[413] chapkan or kaba,[414] and an Amamah turban.[415]
However, he eventually switched to an Assamese outfit
consisting of a silk dhoti, anga[416] and a *tokoniya pag*.[417] In
the morning and evening, he would wear a pajama and a
chapkan at home or on his walks, often accompanied by a
hat. He always made sure to wear socks and shoes. When
taking a shower, he wore a dhoti, and then changed into
a red silk dhoti, woollen or *cheli*[418] garment. Later, he
switched back to a dhoti, which he wore until the morning.
He always wore a flannel vest, except during worship.
Finally, he would wear *kharam*[419] before his shower, which
he changed when dressing after his meal.

Ananda Ram kept a low wooden stool and a rug near
his study table. Visitors were seated on it based on their
social status. For native gentlemen, he had a floor bed with
cushions nearby. He received English gentlemen in another
room, furnished with tables, chairs, and couches, enhanced
by paintings and other decorative items. Ananda Ram

---

[413] A loose-fitting trouser.

[414] A long, loose-fitting coat.

[415] A headwear consisting of a cap with an outer tail.

[416] A long shirt.

[417] A turban with a pointed top.

[418] A kind of silk cloth.

[419] A type of wooden footwear.

would rest in his bedroom or dressing room, where he had a bed, reading books or newspapers. Sometimes, he would even take a quick nap.

Ananda Ram was a man who did not crave luxury. He was satisfied with leading a happy and comfortable life. As his home in Guwahati was in poor condition, he gathered bricks and other materials to construct a new concrete house there just before his death. Additionally, he began building a magnificent sitting hall at the foundation of the old one, which had been damaged by a fire.

Ananda Ram owned four bookcases filled with books on various subjects in English, Sanskrit and other languages. He was very particular about keeping his books and other household items clean and often rearranged them. An expert in interior decoration, he ensured that everything in his house was well organized and classified. At one point, he owned books on law worth Rs 369, and his furniture, including tables, chairs and a couch, cost Rs 1100. He organized his clothes and other items himself and checked on them regularly.

Letter-writing was one of Ananda Ram's main occupations, and he tried to answer every letter he received as soon as possible. Many people wrote to him for various reasons. However, he could not spare much time on letter-writing, as he had to spend most of his time translating legal books. Therefore, he dictated a few of his letters to someone while shaving or taking a shower and then sent them off with his signature.

Ananda Ram was a social person who treated others with respect. He always tried to follow traditions and customs to avoid causing any trouble in society. When he visited the head of Auniati Satra, he was offered a plantain leaf to sit on. Ananda Ram accepted the offer, believing it was his duty to obey the owner's wishes during a visit.

Ananda Ram preferred not to draw attention to himself. He did not mention his name in several of his books, including *Asamiya Lorar Mitra, A Few Remarks on the Assamese Language and on Vernacular Education*[420] and *Sadar Adalater Nispatti.*[421] Even when he wrote *Aain o Byabastha Sangraha,*[422] he only used his initials instead of his full name in the introduction. Eventually, he added his name to the title page after facing pressure from others. Ananda Ram believed in helping people without seeking recognition. He followed the saying of Christ, 'When you give to the needy, do not let your left hand know what your right hand is doing.' He also believed that every action had a result, but one should not have high expectations.

Ananda Ram was concerned about being perceived as uncivilized. He would thoroughly prepare before meeting and speaking with someone. He was highly skilled at engaging in conversations with others. He discussed topics relevant to their professions or social circles, being direct

---

[420] The original text describes it as a book on the Assamese Language (*asamiya bhasha bisayak grantha*).

[421] *A Selection of Sudder Civil Court Judgments.*

[422] *Notes on Laws of Bengal.*

with everyone and providing suggestions when asked for advice. He would never pressure anyone to follow his advice or argue to establish his opinion. He did not mind if people did not take his advice and disliked it when others argued to force their views.

He was very sharp and could offer excellent suggestions, and it was well-known that he could write well-structured drafts. He wrote papers and drafts for Koch Bihar's dewan, Kalichandra Lahiri, and many others. He could ascertain the result of every action or conversation, which was why his opinion mattered to all. Occasionally, he drafted documents for his friends living in faraway places.

He enjoyed conversing with elders and learning about things from the past. Very curious, he always got to the bottom of every matter. Therefore, he was willing to change his views. He met people but disliked spending time in idle talk. He did not open up to people until he knew them well, which led him to be sometimes labelled as arrogant. He never consumed betel nuts or *mola-dhapat*[423] but offered them to his visitors. On the day of Bijoya Dashami,[424] several Bengali officials and Assamese gentlemen would visit his home. He hugged[425] everyone with great pleasure and then talk to them while sitting on the floor bed. Many Assamese and Bengali individuals regularly visited him. Habiram

---

[423] Ground tobacco with molasses.

[424] The last day of Durga Puja.

[425] *Kolakuli*: a ritual where people hug and console each other after bidding farewell to Goddess Durga.

Barua Peshkar, Ratneswar Lahiri, Kalicharan Kanungo, Ramchandra Biswas, Kalikrishna Roy, Monmukh Das, Dhirsi Syal and Soval frequently visited him in Nagaon.

During his father's annual shraddha, performed in the month of Saon, and his sons' *annaprasan*,[426] Ananda Ram arranged traditional feasts for Assamese community. The next day, another Bengali feast was arranged for Bengalis and Hindustanis. He treated everyone equally at these events. He also sent food items to the English and Muslims during these celebrations.

Whenever a family member fell ill or there was an upcoming event at home, he became quite concerned. He took prompt action if someone disobeyed his directives. At such moments, he would become easily agitated but never showed it in front of guests. He would admonish or sometimes reprimand his subordinates for their errors, but never did so in front of strangers.

Ananda Ram disliked any signs of an inferiority complex in others. Once, when a clerk from an ancient noble family referred to him as 'my lord', Ananda Ram, feeling upset, requested the clerk not to do so again. He never boasted about his position as a magistrate. His wife, Mahindri, became a *sokhi*[427] of bailiff Ranjay Phukan's wife, Bhagirathi *aaisu*,[428] and was very close to her. Ananda Ram was perfectly fine with this friendship and never restrained

---

[426] First rice-feeding ritual.

[427] A formally constituted friendship.

[428] A form of addressing the wife of an Ahom noble man.

Mahindri. Ananda Ram could not complete his college education. However, he worked hard upon returning home and made immense progress. He was proficient in English, Bengali and Assamese, and wrote books in all three languages. He also had some knowledge of Urdu and Persian. He could easily understand elementary Sanskrit books. He was very studious and made sure to study every day, often continuing to read or write even while engaged in conversation. His passion for studying was so intense that, at times, he appeared to read aloud even while sleeping. He never gave a public speech, even though he was highly skilled in speaking and writing in English. If one heard him talking to an Englishman, they would think they were listening to a native speaker of English. Similarly, his proficiency in Bengali was such that he sounded like a Calcutta native. He had a basic command of writing in Persian and could communicate in Urdu. He was less proficient in speaking and writing Sanskrit than in the other languages.

Ananda Ram worked very hard for the Assamese language. He refused to use words from Sanskrit or other languages if there was a proper word in Assamese. Unlike other Assamese people who wrote letters in Bengali, Ananda Ram always wrote in Assamese and even answered Bengali letters from Assamese individuals in Assamese. He was committed to propagating the use of the Assamese language and took great care to write appropriately, which was not the common practice at that time.

Ananda Ram hoped to write a history of Assam, following in the footsteps of his father, Haliram, but was

unable to fulfil this wish. His incomplete manuscript of
the *Note on Laws*[429] became disorganized as his family had
to frequently move. Although he only knew the basics of
science and mathematics, along with some understanding
of logic, aesthetics and psychology, he was an expert in
legal studies. His scholarship and capacity for collecting
materials in this subject were evident in his two books,
Sadar Adalater Nispatti and *Aain o Byabastha Sangraha*.

He practised no art forms but had a strong aesthetic
sense. He collaborated with a tailor from Nagaon, Kahpur
and two tailors from Guwahati, Kabur and Raskul, to create
beautiful garments using *karchobi*[430] and other techniques.
This collaboration also served as business development
training for the tailors. Ananda Ram's Assamese turban-
tying method is still praised today.

Ananda Ram was not musically inclined and never
received any training, nor did he ever attempt to attain
it. But he nevertheless appreciated sweet melodies. He
hummed Assamese songs or Sanskrit shlokas whenever
he had spare time and sometimes even whistled the tunes.
Unlike other people, he did not like to read old Assamese
manuscripts of verses, rather he enjoyed listening when
others read them aloud. He enjoyed listening to folk
tales. He never participated in the singing of *naam*[431] but
loved to listen to the melody at bedtime and even asked

---

[429] He intended to write the second volume of *A Note on the Laws
of Bengal.*

[430] A type of embroidery.

[431] Assamese devotional songs in praise of gods and goddesses.

Kambukantha to learn to play the violin. Kambukantha learnt the instrument for a while and would play it during Ananda Ram's bedtime, which left him greatly contented.

Ananda Ram had no knowledge of card games, such as choupat or chess.[432] Even the few games he used to play, he stopped paying attention to after his first visit to Calcutta. He mainly took pleasure in talking to people. He was known for keeping his language clean and never engaged in discussions of an erotic nature. While many people tend to use vulgar language in their youth, Ananda Ram was not one of them. He was not familiar with erotic slangs and never used them in his conversations.

Ananda Ram was a person who refrained from engaging in gossip and slander about others. He despised such things and was not known for having an extreme temper. But one day, a washerman damaged an expensive garment of his, and Ananda Ram hit him on the head with a stick, causing him to bleed. Ananda Ram regretted the incident afterwards.

He despised corruption. During his time as Bijni's dewan, he only accepted what was due to him. In Assamese culture, it is customary to bring a gift when visiting a person of elite standing or an officer, but Ananda Ram did not like this custom and requested that no one bring him any gifts. He even ordered the ladies of the family not to accept such gifts. He did not like accepting gifts from friends and relatives either.

---

[432] Gunabhiram contradicts himself here. He mentions Ananda Ram used to play Choupat as a child in the first chapter.

Ananda Ram did not envy anyone. To this day, no one can say that he had a single enemy. Even the prisoners he had convicted as part of his duty liked him. They mourned his death as if someone from their own family had passed away.

Ananda Ram was a man dedicated to helping others. He took on the responsibility of raising Gunabhiram from a very young age, sent him to study in Calcutta at his own expense and arranged his marriage. He did the same for Kambukantha and Dharmadatta. Ananda Ram also looked after the education and managed the property of Durgachandra and Brajasundari. He helped other compatriots as well by arranging jobs for them. He was always there for the unfortunate, the poor, his friends and relatives, providing whatever they needed. While in Nagaon, he arranged the marriage of one of his dependants every year. He was passionate about the progress of his compatriots and often tried to uplift them.

Ananda Ram regularly visited schools to inspect them and encourage the students. He also motivated the native youth towards progress with his inspiring words. Many Assamese people were inspired by his example and began to write. Whenever he got a chance, Ananda Ram urged government officials to develop Assam. He replied encouragingly to anyone who wrote to him and tried his best to arrange treatment for anyone who fell ill and even paid the bills of poor patients. When the head of Gormur Satra and Ranjay Phukan were diagnosed with untreatable ailments, Ananda Ram arranged for their surgeries by European doctors, which cured them. Usually, people fear medical treatment, but these two, inspired by Ananda

Ram's enthusiasm and care, accepted medical treatment and were cured.

Ananda Ram was a man who held very liberal views. He loved the people of Assam and had no dislike towards the Bengalis. He did not have any prejudices against Bengalis as outcasts. He only disliked people with bad character from both communities. For him, people from all religions, whether Hindus, Muslims or Christians, were equal. He did not judge people based on their religious beliefs and was, in fact, delighted when someone followed their own religion.

Ananda Ram despised hypocrisy and was shocked to learn that one of his friends secretly drank wine while in Calcutta. His character was pure, and he detested immorality. When one of his friends told him that adultery was not a sin, he was bewildered and taken aback. He always felt embarrassed when praised.

His enlightened mind gave birth to many original ideas. One such idea was his proposal to compile a digest of the Sudder court decrees, which had not been thought of before, it seems. Ananda Ram had a low tolerance for vulgarity and was particularly offended by the lewd dances performed during Bohag Bihu in some regions of Nagaon.[433] He took

---

[433] Bohag Bihu is a traditional fertility festival celebrated in Assam, marked by various cultural events, including traditional songs and dances in the month of April. Most elites considered this performance immoral and vulgar until the end of the nineteenth century. Later, the Bihu dance got an image makeover by young Assamese intellectuals, including Lakshminath Bezbaroa, and it is now regarded as central to Assamese culture.

it upon himself to put an end to these performances and even convinced everyone of their harmful nature.

His expertise in conducting trials was exceptional, and he had a unique way of getting to the root of the dispute through his jovial interrogation of witnesses. He always passed his judgment without bias and was never influenced by anyone. During the trial, he would talk to everyone with a smile and never intimidated witnesses. His judgment was always fair, and no request could sway it. He never required any help from anyone, as he would go through all the documents himself. Once, he had to convict a relative in a trial in Nagaon, but he usually did not deliver a severe punishment. Instead, he spared almost every wrongdoer with a light conviction, as he believed they were ignorant. He believed those who feared punishment would correct their behaviour with a light conviction, whereas those not scared of punishment would never change, no matter how severe the punishment.

He was a champion of education and worked hard to set up schools. In fact, he even established an English school in his very own home, as there were no other English schools in Nagaon at the time. A teacher would conduct classes there for students every morning and evening. Thanks to his encouragement, Gunabhiram established a weekly society called Gyan Pradayini.[434] Native gentlemen would gather there every week to discuss various topics.

---

[434] The Imparting of Knowledge.

Ananda Ram had great respect for women's education and even taught his wife himself. He began his daughter Padmavati's education at the age of five. He believed that both men and women were human beings, and that if women went without education, men would be paralysed. Furthermore, he was a strong advocate for women's freedom. He believed that giving freedom to educated women was not a bad thing at all.

Ananda Ram was a man who liked to donate to charity but never overspent. He maintained a budget under different headings, including religious works, donations, children's education and family expenditures. He spent money on a specific cause only from the budget allocated for that category. At his demise, he could only leave a promissory note worth Rs 8500 to his family, a minuscule amount of which came from his income. He cleared his bills almost every month, having minimal unpaid dues.

Ananda Ram was devoted to his parents. He always listened with the utmost respect whenever his father's name was mentioned. He was equally devoted to his mother and stepmother and always made sure of their well-being. A few days before his death, Ananda Ram sat near his mother and exclaimed how time flies. He adored his children but never made them sit on his lap or cuddled them. He loved and cared for his wife very much. They had occasional fights, but these fizzled out very soon. In household matters, he accepted his wife's advice and sometimes his mother's. In case of a disagreement, Ananda Ram could always counsel them well.

Ananda Ram never consumed any intoxicants, including betel nut, tobacco, opium, cannabis or alcohol. He used to have tea after every meal. As he felt weak due to excessive labour, he began to take a small dose of Kameswar Modak.[435] However, he gave up the habit after the Modak made him feel uncomfortable a couple of times. He had only spices, such as cardamom, after his meals.

Ananda Ram was a devout follower of the Vedic religion. His faith only strengthened after he spoke with Reverend Bland, who visited Nagaon shortly before Ananda Ram's passing. Ananda Ram firmly believed that abandoning old customs and embracing Christianity was unnecessary. Despite being labelled a Christian by some, he adamantly stated from his sickbed that he was not one. He believed in God wholeheartedly. He often felt the presence of God and death around him, which only served to strengthen his faith. In many situations, he would utter the phrase 'God willing' and surrender to God.

He was always punctual and made sure he completed everything on time. He maintained a diary, in which he recorded his daily activities. He occasionally went through it to evaluate his progress and setbacks. The following memorable lines were found in his diary:

- Be moderate, hold your tongue, and you will live a long life.

---

[435] Modak is a medicine made from hemp leaves and various herbs and spices, known for its stimulating effects.

- Exercise in the morning and evening.
- Avoid delaying anything you need to do, such as reading, writing, working or writing a letter.
- Remember that time flies by quickly, so utilize your time properly and avoid wasting it.
- It is foolish to wait for the perfect time and a comfortable life to start your religious practices. We never know how much time we have left in this life.
- Do not let your busy schedule interfere with your devotion to God. Everything else comes second to worshipping God. Worry for nothing in this life and prioritize your duties accordingly.
- Promise to be enthusiastic about religion and helping others every day. Be steady and start with double the energy. By the end of the day, you should feel the effect of your words and actions like a petition for an appeal.
- Do not forget to pray at these times: after waking up, after your bath, in the evening, before bed, while in bed and whenever you read this.
- Remember how you feel when people around you suffer from cholera.
- Keep track of the prayer schedules of Christians, Muslims and Hindus. Fast on Ekadashi.
- Be prepared for death because we never know when it will come; it could be in a day or a week.
- Let us think of Him who controls the soul of the bright sun and our mind.

Who would not deeply admire and respect Ananda Ram when one remembers these memorable quotes? He truly embodied and followed his own thoughts of worshipping God and completing one's work in this life. In addition to his daily prayers, he also prayed to his deity after every meal. He always fulfilled his duties and never postponed them, which saved his family from chaos after his death. Ananda Ram was adored and respected by all for his sharp intellect, impeccable character, honesty and his works for the benefit of the people. Even today, he is considered an exemplar of good character and deeds. Although he had to leave this temporary world by God's will and move on to his permanent heavenly abode, his memory will remain everlasting in this world.

Epilogue

Ananda Ram's family stayed in Nagaon for a year after his passing. In October 1859, Gunabhiram was appointed sub-assistant commissioner and moved to Tezpur. Later, in January 1860, he was transferred to Goalpara. Mahindri moved to Guwahati with her family during the monsoon of 1860 but had to shift to Goalpara because the old house was uncomfortable and the new one was not ready yet. Dharmadatta began building the new house. Unfortunately, everyone in Goalpara fell ill, and they returned to Guwahati in October 1860. Ananda Ram's mother passed away the following month. Padmavati married Sashadhar Phukan's son, Nandishwar[436] in December 1862. After a few months, during the monsoon of 1863, Chandraprabha passed away. Radhika and Annada started attending the English school in Guwahati.

In early 1864, Mahindri travelled to Murshidabad for a ritual bathing in the Ganga, while Radhika, Annada and Padmavati stayed with Gunabhiram in Barpeta.

---

[436] The original text mentioned that they belong to Shulapani Bharali Barua's family.

Gunabhiram had to move to Goalpara again, and Radhika and Annada returned to Guwahati to continue their schooling. By the beginning of 1866, Gunabhiram was transferred to Nagaon. Radhika's sacred thread ceremony, where Balaram presented him with the sacred thread, was celebrated shortly after. Meanwhile, their Nagaon land and house were sold to Singer.[437]

Gunabhiram's wife, Brajasundari, had suffered several stillbirths in the past. When Gunabhiram was transferred to Dhuburi in July 1868, Brajasundari stayed back in Nagaon. Unfortunately, she passed away in the same month after giving birth to another stillborn child.

After his marriage, Nandishwar went to Calcutta but returned to his hometown in early 1866. During the monsoon of 1867, he took Padmavati to his workplace in Tezpur after performing the ritual of the second marriage.[438] Mahindri passed away in December 1867, leaving her two sons orphaned. At that time, a significant amount of expensive jewellery was stolen. Nandishwar and Padmavati moved to Guwahati in early 1868 to look after the boys.

Mahindri was a highly intelligent and efficient homemaker, known for her kindness. She was considered one of the most distinguished and educated ladies of her time.

Shortly after the devastating earthquake of January 1869, Annadaram underwent the sacred thread ceremony,

---

[437] Lieutenant G B Singer was the Assistant Commissioner in Nagaon.

[438] *Shanti Bibah.* See Chapter 1.

where Radhika presented him with the sacred thread. In early 1871, Radhika went to Calcutta after passing his entrance examination in 1870 with second division. However, he could not clear the intermediate[439] examination and returned to Guwahati in 1872. Later, he returned to Calcutta and left for England on 17 June 1873 to study law.

In February–March, 1860,[440] Balaram Phukan married the daughter of Goswami from Jakhalabandha Jamuguri. His first wife gave birth to their eldest son, Jivanram, in October–November 1860.[441] Jivanram had six siblings— Nabinram, Bipinram, Tarunram, Manamohini, Jagyaseni and Girijaya. Balaram's second wife had only one daughter named Padmarekha. Manamohini married Durgachandra, and they have a son named Abhay. Jagyaseni was married to Ramanath Kataki, and they have a daughter. Jivanram and Nabinram married the eldest and youngest daughters of Kambukantha. Balaram leads an independent life by managing his estates, elephant trade and other enterprises. His three elder sons are currently studying in schools, while Padmarekha has been married to one of Kameswar Baruah's sons.

Prithuram Barua, the son of Sambhuram, had three sons named Kaliram, Kashiram and Raghuram. Kaliram worked in the education department, while Kashiram worked in the revenue department in Kamrup. Sitaram

---

[439] First Arts (FA) examination.

[440] Fagun, 1782 Sak.

[441] Kati, 1783 Sak.

Barua's daughter had a widowed granddaughter. Abhiram Barua's grandson lives in Goalpara district.

Gunabhiram was transferred to Goalpara from Dhuburi in April 1869. He was concerned about the harm caused by the non-recognition of widow remarriage in this province, even back in his student days, and was inclined to support widow marriage. He was also inclined towards the Brahmo religion ever since his Calcutta days, although he did not convert to it openly. He converted in Dhuburi in 1869 and married Bishnupriya Devi, the widow of Parashuram Barua. Parashuram was a friend of Ananda Ram's and had married Bishnupriya, the middle daughter of Lambodar Kataki, in 1853. He passed away in 1863, leaving two daughters named Kalipriya and Damayanti.

In 1871, Gunabhiram was transferred to Nagaon, where he has lived ever since. Gunabhiram and Bishnupriya had a daughter named Swarnalata, born in February 1871, who has now started studying at Calcutta's Bethune school. They also had a son named Karunabhiram, born on 2 June 1874, and another son named Kamalabhiram, born on 14 March 1878. In 1872, they had one more son, named Satyabhiram, who died in 1873 in Nagaon. Gunabhiram had another son named Gyanadabhiram, born on 19 August 1880. His marriage with Bishnupriya was registered under Act III of 1872 in December of the same year.

Ananda Ram's stepmother passed away in 1866. His sister Tuloshi lives with her husband, Raghudev Goswami, the head of Jakhalabandha Satra. They have three sons named Chandrahas, Ghanahas and Gunahas, and three daughters named Sabitri, Subhadra and Haripriya. They also had two more sons, Padmahas and Tarahas, who are no longer alive. Sabitri and Subhadra are now married. Chandrahas is also married and has a son named Jagatchandra.

Padmavati has four sons and two daughters. Among them, three sons—Navakumar, Chandrakumar and Saratkumar—have already passed away. Padmavati now has one son, Prasannakumar, and two daughters, Hemangini and Sarojini. Nandishwar works as a superintendent in the revenue department in Nagaon and lives there with his family.

Annadaram went to Calcutta in September 1871 and returned in 1874. He could not clear the matriculation examination. After returning, he married Golapi, also known as Golokeswari, the eldest daughter of Purnanada Barua, in August 1875. They were blessed with a son named Master Debendraram in 1878. Annadaram has been living independently, engaged in the tea trade and other general enterprises. Radhikaram has yet to return from England. Everyone hopes he will return soon, without any glitches, after securing success.

The Family Tree of Ananda Ram Dhekial Phookan

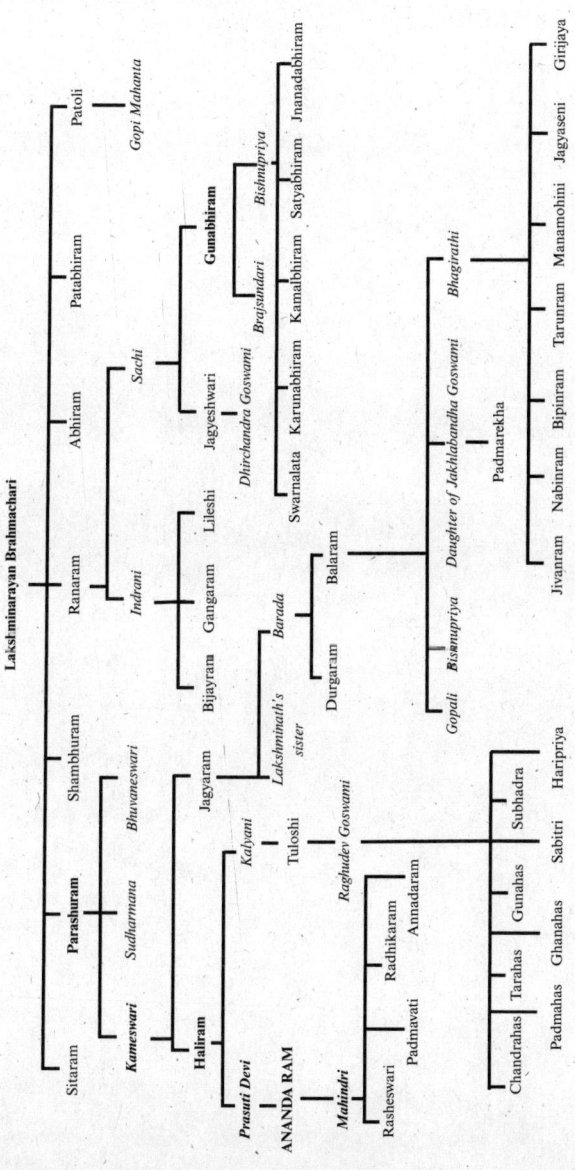

Chronological Order of Events
(1779–1880)

1779: Gourinath Singha becomes the king (Swargadeo) of Assam.

1792: Civil rebellion erupts in Assam, led by the Moamoriyas. Captain Thomas Welsh of the English East India Company leads a military campaign to Assam in September to support the Ahom king against the Moamoriya rebels. Laksminarayan Brahmachari arrives in Assam and adopts six children.

1794 Kamaleswar Singha becomes the king of Assam.

1799: Laksminarayan becomes the Duworiya Barua (customs officer) at Hadirachoki in western Assam.

1811 Chandrakanta Singha becomes the king of Assam.

1816: First Burmese invasion of the Ahom kingdom; Burmese forces withdraw in April 1817.

1819:   Second Burmese invasion of Assam; Chadrakanta Singha is reinstalled as king of Assam under Burmese control; The Burmese maintain effective control of Assam until 1824.

1823:   David Scott appointed as Agent to the Governor-General for the Eastern Frontier of Bengal in November.

1824:   The English East India Company government in Bengal launches a military campaign against the Burmese forces in Assam.

1826:   Treaty of Yandabo signed between East India Company and the Burmese King; Burmese military withdraws from Assam, and the East India Company assumes control of the region.

1827–28: Jagyaram Phukan travels to Calcutta to study under Rammohan Roy.

1828:   David Scott redesignated as Commissioner of Revenue and Circuit of Assam in December, while retaining his position as Agent.

1829:   Publication of Haliram Dhekial Phukan's *Asam Buranji* from Calcutta's Samachar Chandrika Press; Birth of Ananda Ram Dhekial Phookan to Haliram Dhekial Phukan and Prasuti Devi.

1831:   Haliram Dhekial Phukan passes away.

1835:   Establishment of English and Bengali medium schools in Guwahati.

1837:   Introduction of the Assam Code for regulation of procedures in civil and criminal cases.

1839:   Formation of the Assam Company in London, which begins tea plantation operations in Assam.

1841:   Ananda Ram and Durgaram travel to Calcutta for higher studies at Hindu College.

1843:   First introduction of regular land assessment system in Assam.

1844-1845: Ananda Ram returns to Guwahati.

1846:   Launch of *Orunodoi*, the first Assamese magazine (published monthly); Ananda Ram begins contributing to it.

1847:   Introduction of steamer service between Calcutta and Guwahati on the Brahmaputra River

1847:   Ananda Ram appointed as acting Munshef at Nalbari in November.

1849:   Publication of Ananda Ram's *Asamiya Lorar Mitra* from Calcutta. Ananda Ram becomes Dewan of Bijni zamindari estate.

1850:   Ananda Ram begins publishing court judgments in Bengali. Appointed as acting Sub-Assistant Commissioner of Nagaon.

1852:   Ananda Ram attends the inaugural meeting of the Bethune Society in Calcutta in January.

1852:   Ananda Ram takes a daguerreotype photograph. Establishes New Press at Calcutta under Gunabhiram's name. Appointed as Sub-Assistant Commissioner in Barpeta.

1853:   Ananda Ram submits a comprehensive memorandum to the touring Judge of Sudder Court at Calcutta, outlining a future development roadmap for Assam.

1854:   At Nagaon, Ananda Ram is granted the powers of a junior assistant and a Sadar Amin.

1855:   Ananda Ram proposes building a channel to connect the Kolong (a distributary of the Brahmaputra) and Brahmaputra river; vaccinates his children; publishes *A Few Remarks on the Assamese Language and on Vernacular Education in Assam*. Also publishes *A Note on the Laws of Bengal*, vol. 1 from Calcutta's New Press.

1857:   The Sepoy Mutiny spreads across North and Central India. In Assam, Maniram Dewan collaborates with Kandarpeswar Singha to plan a local uprising; both are tried for treason, with Maniram subsequently executed by hanging.

1858:   Ananda Ram conducts river engineering experiments on the Kolong; famine outbreak in Nagaon district; the British Crown assumes direct control of India from the East India Company; Phookan initiates his first savings programme.

1859:   Ananda Ram passes away.

1859:   Gunabhiram begins serial publication of Ananda Ram's biography in *Orunodoi*.

1873:   Assamese officially recognized as the administrative language of Assam. Ananda Ram's son Radhikaram went to England for higher studies.

1874:   Assam designated as a Chief Commissioner's Province.

1880:   Publication of *Anandaram Dhekial Phookanar Jivan Charitra* from Calcutta.

Scan QR code to access the
Penguin Random House India website